Bob Benton and Daniel Brodie
for DB Productions
in association with Park Theatre
present

The Patriotic Traitor

by Jonathan Lynn

EAST SUSSEX COUNTY COUNCIL
WITHDRAWN
0 7 JUN 2024
17

D1136206

The Cast

in alphabetical order

Canon Pottevin, Cadet, Deladier,
POW Officer, Léon Blum, Laval
Niall Ashdown

Cadet, General le Gallet, POW Officer,
Payen, De Courcel, Pomaret
James Chalmers

Philippe Pétain
Tom Conti

Charles de Gaulle
Laurence Fox

Yvonne de Gaulle
Ruth Gibson

General Joffre, General Herring,
General Weygand, Lord Halifax
Tom Mannion

All other roles played by members of the cast

The play takes place in Paris, London, Vichy
and Colombey-les-Deux-Eglises, between 1913 and 1945

Creative Team

Writer and Director	**Jonathan Lynn**
Designer	**Georgia Lowe**
Lighting Designer	**Mark Howland**
Sound Designer	**Andrea J. Cox**
Costume Supervisor	**Jackie Orton**
Assistant Director	**Martha Geelan**
Production Manager	**David Leigh-Pemberton**
Company Stage Manager	**Hannah Gore**
Stage Manager	**Andrew McCabe**
Costume	**Angels the Costumiers**
Press	**Arabella Neville-Rolfe** for Target Live
Graphic Designer	**Rebecca Pitt**
Production Photographer	**Helen Murray**
Production Accountants	**Keith Cunningham** and **Inda Bunyan**
General Management	**Daniel Brodie** for Daniel Brodie Productions and **Freddie Ryecart** for Bob and Co
Producers	**Bob Benton** and **Daniel Brodie** for DB Productions

Thanks to

Matthew Dewsbury, Jamie Hendry Productions,
Alan Brodie, Alison Lee and Kate Brower at Alan Brodie
Representation, Lloyd Thomas, Pooles Park Primary School,
Ashleigh Cheadle, the many PATRIOTIC supporters
and everyone at Park Theatre.

Cast Biographies

Niall Ashdown

Theatre credits include: *Tristan and Yseult* (Kneehigh Theatre/US tour), *Impropera* (Kings Place); *Never Try This at Home* (Birmingham Rep/Told By An Idiot); *Public Enemy, Annie Get Your Gun* (Young Vic); *Accidental Death of an Anarchist* (Bolton Octagon); *The Ratcatcher of Hamelin, The 1966 World Cup Final, The Man Who Would Be Sting, Hungarian Bird Festival, Animo* (BAC); *Lifegame* (Imbrobable Theatre/international tour); *The Hunchback of Notre Dame* (West Yorkshire Playhouse); *An Evening with Gary Lineker* (Duchess Theatre); *Improbable Tales* (Nottingham Playhouse). He is a regular guest with *The Comedy Store Players*, Paul Merton's *Impro Chums* and *Ross Noble and Friends*.

Television includes: *Dark Angel, Parents, Outnumbered, The Littlest Boho, After You've Gone, Angel Cake, Barking, Royalty Bloopers, Whose Line Is It Anyway?, Confessions, Drop the Dead Donkey.*

Radio includes: *The Arabian Nights, Tunnel Vision, Hungarian Birdsong, Losers, The Motion Show, The Worriers, The Treatment, The Back Page, Life, Death and Sex, Kalangadog Junction, North-East of Eden.*

Writing includes: *Nick Hancock's World of Sport, Losers, Barking, The Treatment, Good Cop/Bad Cop, Speaking Volumes, Confessions.*

James Chalmers

James trained at LAMDA.

Theatre credits include: *Tamar's Revenge, The Dog in the Manger, Pedro the Great Pretender, House of Desires, Trouble and Wonder, The Irish Play* (RSC, Madrid and West End); *An Evening of High Drung and Slarrit, America Hurrah, A Resounding Tinkle, I Love Satan* (Royal Court); *The Lie/It Is There, Measure for Measure* (RNT Studio); *Othello, Richard III* (Guildford Shakespeare Company); *The War in Heaven* (Rose Theatre); *The Daughter in Law* (Watford Palace Theatre); *Romeo and Juliet* (Northcott Theatre); *Warm, If So Then Yes* (Presence Theatre); *Sleeping Around* (Jermyn Street Theatre); *The Code Breaker* (Apollo Theatre), *The Matchmaker* (international tour).

Television includes: *The Vice, The Bill, Casualty, Doctors, EastEnders.*

Film includes: *Daisy, Within the Woods, The Good Life, Thin the Herd, The Rights of a Soldier, Overlord, Siren, Vocation, Monitor.*

Tom Conti

I could have been a helluva plumber. My mother, upon my rejection of all professions in favour of acting, said two things: 'Remember, people always need a plumber,' and 'You need a haircut.' Out of work, I have sometimes stared at a dripping tap and wondered how it might have been. People in my business wade through a lot of sewage; you watch your fair share of it.

In my first week at drama school, I met John Groves, who had a fierce reputation. His opening line was 'Acting or teaching?' 'Acting.' He gave me a carpet brush, a 12x1 piece of timber and a bucket. 'There's a blocked drain in the lane. I don't want to see you till it's clear.' The cover had not been off for decades. With help from my penknife, it lifted. I pushed the 12x1 into the gunge hoping it would miraculously clear. Nope. Why the carpet brush, God knows and, as usual, wasn't telling, so back for better tools.

'Done it?' 'No but . . .' 'Do it!' Only one way; sleeves up and plunge. From the smell alone, I wished I'd become an accountant. Finally, a pile of ordure beside the drain. 'Done it?' 'Yes, sir.' 'Enjoy it?' 'Not really.' His eyes softened. 'Well, son, that – is the theatre.' For years, it was. Sometimes still is. His mantra? 'Talent is nothing without technique.' If you don't learn? There's always plumbing.

Tom Conti holds an Olivier Award, a Broadway Tony and an Oscar nomination. He and Judi Dench were once voted the Most Popular Actors in the West End in the last twenty-five years. His debut novel *The Doctor* was published in 2004. His next one is just finished.

Laurence Fox

Theatre credits include: *Strangers on a Train* (Gielgud Theatre), *Our Boys* (Duchess Theatre), *Treats* (Garrick Theatre), *'Tis Pity She's a Whore* (Southwark Playhouse) and *Mrs Warren's Profession* (Strand).

Film includes: *W.E.* directed by Madonna, *Blackwater Transit* directed by Tony Kaye, *Elizabeth: The Golden Age* directed by Shekhar Kapur, *Becoming Jane* directed by Julian Jarrold, *Wasp* directed by Woody Allen, *The Last Drop* directed by Colin Teague, *South From Grenada* directed by Fernando Colomo, *Deathwatch* directed by Michael J Bassett, *Gosford Park* directed by Robert Altman and *The Hole* directed by Nick Hamm.

Television includes: *Lewis* (nine series), *Fast Freddie, Wired, A Room with a View, Miss Marple, Whatever Love Means, Egypt, Jericho, Colditz, Ad, BC: A Rock Opera, Island at War* and *Foyle's War*.

Laurence has also successfully launched his music career this year and recently released his debut single 'Headlong' from his album *Holding Patterns*, out on 5 February 2016 through Caroline International. The album will be preceded by the release of his second single 'Rise Again'.

Ruth Gibson

Theatre includes: *The Dead Monkey* (Park Theatre); *Theatre Uncut* (Soho and national tour); *Intimate Exchanges* (Mercury Theatre); *The Kitchen* (National Theatre); *Portmanteau* (Arcola Theatre); *My Wonderful Day* (Stephen Joseph Theatre, New York, and national tour, nominated for Drama Desk Best Play Award); *Snake in the Grass, Life and Beath, Touchwood, Forget Me Not Lane* (SJT); *Man of the Moment, Private Fears in Public Places* (Theatre Royal, Northampton); *Independent Means* (Library Theatre, MEN Best Actress Award); *Vieux Carré* (Library Theatre); *Anne of Green Gables* (Sadler's Wells); *After Mrs Rochester* (Duke of York's Theatre, Evening Standard Best Play Award); *Blood Brothers* (Phoenix Theatre); and *Sonnets* (Shakespeare's Globe).

TV includes: *Babylon; The Littlest Boho; Doctors; Judge John Deed* and *The Culture Show*.

Film includes: *Moomins On the Riviera* and *Good Girl Bad Girl*.

Tom Mannion

Tom trained at the Royal Scottish Academy of Music and Drama

Theatre credits include: *All My Sons, The Two Gentlemen of Verona, Bartholomew Fair, Much Ado about Nothing* (Regents Park Open Air Theatre), *An Inspector Calls* (national tour), *The Ancient Secret of Youth* and *The Five Tibetans, The Price* (Octagon, Bolton), *A Midsummer Night's Dream* (Globe), *The Cherry Orchard* (Sheffield Crucible), *Hamlet* (Old Vic), *Coriolanus, The Merry Wives of Windsor, Julius Caesar* (RSC), *Art* (Wyndham's), *Closer* (West End), *The Threepenny Opera* (Donmar), *Cyrano de Bergerac* (national tour).

Radio includes: *Macbeth, Pericles, Birdsong, The Archers.*

Television includes: *Inside Men, Spooks, Taggart, Life on Mars, Hustle, Lip Service.*

Creative Team Biographies

Jonathan Lynn

Jonathan Lynn's London theatre debut was as Motel the Tailor in the original West End cast of *Fiddler on the Roof*. His London directing credits include *The Glass Menagerie*, *Songbook* (Best Musical – Olivier Award and Evening Standard Award), *Anna Christie* (RSC, Stratford and Donmar), *The Unvarnished Truth*, *Loot*, Eric Idle's *Pass the Butler*, *Arms and the Man*, *Tonight at Eight-Thirty*, David Wood's *The Plotters of Cabbage Patch Corner* and *The Gingerbread Man* (twice, at the Old Vic). At the National Theatre: Feydeau's *A Little Hotel on the Side* translated by John Mortimer, *Jacobowsky and the Colonel* and *Three Men on a Horse* (Olivier Award, Best Comedy). As Artistic Director of the Cambridge Theatre Company (1977–81) he directed nineteen productions, including *Macbeth* and *The Relapse*, and produced twenty others. Nine of these shows transferred to London.

He has directed ten feature films, and written three (*Clue*, *Nuns on the Run* and *The Internecine Project*). His many TV performances include the memorable plays *Barmitzvah Boy*, *The Knowledge* and *Outside Edge*. He has written dozens of episodes of TV comedy series and is best known for the multi-award winning *Yes Minister* and *Yes Prime Minister*, created and written with Antony Jay. He co-wrote and directed the stage play *Yes Prime Minister* and wrote the best-selling books *The Complete Yes Minister* and *The Complete Yes Prime Minister*, still in print after more than thirty years. He also wrote *Mayday*, a novel, and *Comedy Rules*, a sort of memoir.

Georgia Lowe

Georgia trained on the Motley Theatre Design course and was a Linbury Prize for Stage Design finalist 2011.

Recent designs include: *Yen* (Royal Court); *In the Night Time* (Before The Sun Rises, Gate Theatre); *Pomona* (National Theatre/Royal Exchange); *Four Fridas* (Greenwich & Docklands International Festival); *Defect* (Arts Educational Schools); *These Trees are Made of Blood* (Southwark Playhouse); *Yen* (Royal Exchange, Manchester); *Need a Little Help* (Tangled Feet); *Pomona* (Orange Tree Theatre); *Far Away* (Young Vic); *Bluebeard's Castle* (Opera de Oviedo); *Last Words You'll Hear* (Almeida Theatre/Latitude Festival); *Turfed* (LIFT Festival); *Alarms and Excursions* (Chipping Norton); *Eldorado* (Arcola Studio); *The Mystae* and *Ignorance* (Hampstead Theatre Downstairs, Unicorn); *Unscorched*, *Facts*, *Fog* and *Blue Surge* (Finborough Theatre); *The Ruling Class* (English Theatre Frankfurt); *Commonwealth* (Almeida Projects); *Acis and Galatea* (Iford Arts); *Say It with Flowers* (Sherman Cymru); *Lift* (Soho Theatre); *Pericles* (RSC); *Promise* (Arts Ed); *Handel's Susanna* (Iford Arts); *After the Rainfall* (Curious Directive); *The Dark Side of Love* (RSC/Lift/World Shakespeare Festival); *Song of Songs* (RSC); *Shallow Slumber* (Soho Theatre); *Yellow* (Tête à Tête Opera); *Drowning on Dry Land* (Jermyn Street Theatre) and *Amphibians* (Bridewell Theatre).

Mark Howland

Mark studied, briefly, at Oxford University prior to training in Stage Lighting Design at RADA.

Recent lighting designs include: *The Tales of Hoffmann, Werther, Pelleas et Melisande, La Boheme, Wild Man of the West Indies, The Siege of Calais* (English Touring Opera); *Twelve Angry Men* (Birmingham Rep, West End); *Rodelinda* (Scottish Opera); *Canvas* (Chichester Festival); *The Winters Tale, She Stoops to Conquer, An August Bank Holiday Lark, The Grand Gesture* (Northern Broadsides); *Brassed Off* (York Theatre Royal); *Christians, Image of an Unknown Woman, Edge of Our Bodies, Grounded, Purple Heart, Trojan Women, The Prophet, Yerma, Wittenberg, The Kreutzer Sonata, Vanya* (Gate Theatre, London); *A Further Education, Elephants, Four Minutes Twelve Seconds, The Blackest Black, Ignorance* (Hampstead Theatre); *Pride and Prejudice the Musical, The Man Jesus, Uncle Vanya, Dockers, The Home Place* (Lyric Theatre, Belfast); *Macbeth, Cendrillon* (Blackheath Opera); *Dancing at Lughnasa, Ghosts, Sweeney Todd* (Aarhus Theatre, Denmark); *Singin' in the Rain* (Det Ny Teater, Copenhagen); *Entertaining Mr Sloane, One Flew Over the Cuckoo's Nest, Absurd Person Singular, Molly Sweeney, Translations* (Curve Theatre, Leicester); *The Ladykillers, Hitchcock Blonde* (Hull Truck); *Measure for Measure* (Sherman Cymru); *Six Dance Lessons in Six Weeks* (Vienna's English Theatre); *Bea, Pressure Drop, On Religion* (On Theatre); *Parallel the Suit, Parallel Electra* (Young Vic); *Dick Turpin's Last Ride, Much Ado About Nothing, The London Merchant, Cider with Rosie, The Merchant of Venice* (Theatre Royal, Bury St Edmunds); *A Number* (Salisbury Playhouse); *Topless Mum* (Tobacco Factory); *The Pains of Youth* (Belgrade Theatre).

Andrea J. Cox

Andrea studied Physics and Philosophy at Liverpool University. She has designed shows and worked for the Liverpool Everyman Theatre, Bristol Old Vic and most extensively for the Royal Shakespeare Company.

Recent Theatre sound designs include: *The Harvest* (Ustinov Studio, Bath, Soho Theatre), *Jekyll and Hyde* (UK tour for SellaDoor), *The Shoemaker's Holiday* (Royal Shakespeare Company), *Play Strindberg* (Ustinov Studio, Bath), *True West* (Tricycle Theatre/Glasgow Citizens), *Holes* (Arcola, Edinburgh Fringe), *The Big Meal* (Ustinov Studio, Bath/HighTide Festival), *Alarms and Excursions* (Chipping Norton), *Threeway* (Edinburgh Fringe), *Charlotte's Web – the Musical* (Derby), *Rough Justice* (UK tours), *Sex with a Stranger* (Trafalgar Studios), *Yes, Prime Minister* (Chichester/tours/West End/Los Angeles), *Onassis* (Derby/West End), associate designer on *Calendar Girls* (Chichester and tour), *Pieces* (Clwyd Theatr Cymru/59E59 New York), *A Christmas Carol, A Doll's House, A Midwinter Dream* and *Comedy Chekhovs* (Bridge House Theatre, Warwick), *The Oresteia Trilogy* (Fisher Center, New York), *The Scarecrow and His Servant* (Southwark Playhouse), *Sons of York* (Finborough), *The Pull of Negative Gravity* (Colchester/ Edinburgh/59E59 New York).

Over fifty sound designs for the Royal Shakespeare Company include: *The Histories* (all eight plays from *Richard II* to *Richard III*), *Twelfth Night, The Winter's Tale, Antony and Cleopatra, Measure for Measure, Macbeth, Hamlet,*

The Comedy of Errors, The Duchess of Malfi, Troilus and Cressida, The Theban Plays, Elgar's Rondo, Little Eyolf, Tales from Ovid, Henry VI and *Richard III* (Power Centre, Michigan USA/Young Vic), *As You Like It* (Kennedy Centre, Washington DC), *Ghosts, Henry VI, The Phoenician Women, The Mysteries, Shadows, Bad Weather, A Warwickshire Testimony, The Servant of Two Masters* (Young Vic/West End).

Future projects include: *The Mystery Plays* (York Minster).

Bob Benton

Bob Benton, the founder of Bob & Co, has played a pivotal role in various aspects of the media industry for over twenty years in both advisory roles and the market itself. Bob recently served as Chairman of HandMade Films overseeing the necessary restructuring and sale of the company. His career includes many years' experience in investment banking and stockbroking; positions held include Managing Director and Head of Media at Canaccord Adams and Chief Executive of Ingenious Securities. Prior to that he was Chairman of Bridgewell Group, the stockbroker that he founded in 2002 and floated on the AIM in 2007.

Bob Benton has also held office as Chairman and CEO of Charterhouse Securities, Global Head of Sales at ABN Amro and Managing Director of HSBC Securities Services (formerly HSBC James Capel), before becoming Chief Executive of the company aged 34.

Bob has held a number of investment positions in theatre projects over the last three years including *Beautiful: The Carole King Musical* (both on Broadway and in the West End), *Skylight* (Wyndham's), *Hetty Feather* (Duchess Theatre), *The Play That Goes Wrong* (Duchess Theatre), *The Ladykillers* (Vaudeville), *The Importance of Being Earnest* (Vaudeville) and *Jeeves and Worcester in Perfect Nonsense* (Duke of York's).

Daniel Brodie

Daniel is a freelance theatre producer and has ten years' experience in theatre. Through Daniel Brodie Productions (DBP), he has managed both commercial and subsidised projects for the Royal Court Theatre, Tricycle Theatre, Eclipse Theatre Company, Ambassador Theatre Group and Mongrel Thumb. DBP also produces shows independently. These include: *Facts* by Arthur Milner at the Finborough Theatre, and the four-time Offie nominated *Brenda* by E V. Crowe, at the HighTide Festival and Yard Theatre.

About Park Theatre

Park Theatre was founded by Artistic Director, Jez Bond. The building opened in May 2013 and, with two West End transfers, two national theatre transfers and three national tours in its first two years, quickly garnered a reputation as key player in the London theatrical scene. In 2015 Park Theatre received an Olivier nomination and won The Stage's Fringe Venue of the Year award.

Park Theatre is a neighbourhood theatre with a global ambition.

We present world-class theatre, collaborating with the finest existing and emerging talent. We programme classics through to new writing, distinguished by strong narrative drive and powerful emotional content. We produce both in-house and in partnership with the most excellent existing and emerging producers, with whom we endeavour to provide an unparalleled level of support.

With a welcoming and nurturing environment, we want Park Theatre to be accessible to everyone, within our diverse community and beyond – and through affordable ticket pricing and outreach programmes we aim to engage with those with little or no experience of theatre.

We aim to be a beacon for all and an ambassador for theatre worldwide.

' A five-star neighbourhood theatre.'
Independent

As a registered charity [no.1137223] with no public subsidy, we rely on the kind support of our donors and volunteers.
To find out how you can get involved visit
parktheatre.co.uk

With thanks to all of our supporters,
donors and volunteers.

For Park Theatre

Artistic Director	**Jez Bond**
Executive Director	**John-Jackson (JJ) Almond**
Creative Director	**Melli Bond**
Development Director	**Dorcas Morgan**
Assistant to the Directors	**Amy Lumsden**
Finance Manager	**Catherine Barrow**
Venue and Volunteer Manager	**Naomi Dixon**
Sales and Marketing Manager	**Alona Fogel**
Box Office Manager	**Androulla Erotokritou**
Box Office Supervisors	**Mark Blythe, Bessie Hitchin, Katy Shearstone and Regan Shepherd**
Technical Manager	**Sacha Queiroz**
Theatre and Buildings Technician	**Mat Eldridge-Smith**
Duty Venue Managers	**Mark Blythe, Barry Card, Rochelle Clarke, Androulla Erotokritou and Haroula Lountzi**
Creative Intern	**Wanda Szwed**
Café Bar General Manager	**Tom Bailey**
Bar Staff	**Luis Aguiar, Gemma Barnett, Grace Botang, Calum Budd-Brophy, Jack Carroll, Amy Conway, James Crocker, Robert Czibi, Nicola Grant, Philip Honeywell, Jules Moore-Cook, Joshua Oaks-Rogers, Olivia Onyehara, Sara Pau, Emma Petrusson. Katy Shearstone**
Public Relations	**Arabella Neville-Rolfe** and **Andrew Greer** for Target-Live
President	**Jeremy Bond**
Ambassadors	**David Horovitch, Celia Imrie, Sean Mathias, Tanya Moodie, Hattie Morahan, Tamzin Outhwaite**
Associate Artists	**Mark Cameron, Olivia Poulet, Sarah Rutherford** (Writer in Residence), **Charlie Ward**
Trustees	**Nick Frankfort, Colin Hayfield, Robert Hingley, Rachel Lewis, Mars Lord, Chris McGill, Frank McLoughlin, Nigel Pantling** (Chair), **Jo Parker, Leah Schmidt** (Vice Chair)

The Patriotic Traitor

Jonathan Lynn's London theatre debut was as Motel the Tailor in the original West End cast of *Fiddler on the Roof*. His London directing credits include *The Glass Menagerie*, *Songbook* (Best Musical – Olivier Award and Evening Standard Award), *Anna Christie* (RSC, Stratford and Donmar), *The Unvarnished Truth*, *Loot*, Eric Idle's *Pass the Butler*, *Arms and the Man*, *Tonight at Eight-Thirty*, David Wood's *The Plotters of Cabbage Patch Corner* and *The Gingerbread Man* (twice, at the Old Vic). At the National Theatre: Feydeau's *A Little Hotel on the Side* translated by John Mortimer, *Jacobowsky and the Colonel* and *Three Men on a Horse* (Olivier Award, Best Comedy). As Artistic Director of the Cambridge Theatre Company (1977–81) he directed nineteen productions, including *Macbeth* and *The Relapse*, and produced twenty others. Nine of these shows transferred to London.

He has directed ten feature films and written three (*Clue*, *Nuns on the Run* and *The Internecine Project*). His many TV performances include the memorable plays *Barmitzvah Boy*, *The Knowledge* and *Outside Edge*. He has written dozens of episodes of TV comedy series and is best known for the multi-award winning *Yes Minister* and *Yes Prime Minister*, created and written with Antony Jay. He co-wrote and directed the stage play *Yes Prime Minister* and wrote the best-selling books *The Complete Yes Minister* and *The Complete Yes Prime Minister*, still in print after more than thirty years. He also wrote *Mayday*, a novel, and *Comedy Rules*, a sort of memoir.

also by Jonathan Lynn from Faber

for the stage
YES PRIME MINISTER
(*with Antony Jay*)

prose
COMEDY RULES

JONATHAN LYNN

The Patriotic Traitor

FABER & FABER

First published in 2016
by Faber and Faber Limited
74–77 Great Russell Street, London WC1B 3DA

Reprinted with minor revisions 2016

All rights reserved
© Jonathan Lynn, 2016

The right of Jonathan Lynn to be identified as author
of this work has been asserted in accordance with Section 77
of the Copyright, Designs and Patents Act 1988

Extracts from *Le Fil de l'épée* © Charles de Gaulle, 1932
Reprinted by permission from Editions Plon, 12 Avenue d'Italie,
75627 Paris Cedex 13, France (www.plon.fr)

All rights whatsoever in this work, amateur or professional, are
strictly reserved. Applications for permission for any use whatsoever,
including performance rights, must be made in advance, prior to
any such proposed use, to Alan Brodie Representation Ltd,
Paddock Suite, The Courtyard, 55 Charterhouse Street,
London EC1M 6HA (info@alanbrodie.com)

No performance may be given unless a licence has first been obtained

Typeset by Country Setting, Kingsdown, Kent CT14 8ES
Printed in England by CPI Group (UK) Ltd, Croydon CR0 4YY

*This book is sold subject to the condition that it shall not,
by way of trade or otherwise, be lent, resold, hired out
or otherwise circulated without the publisher's prior consent
in any form of binding or cover other than that in which
it is published and without a similar condition including
this condition being imposed on the subsequent purchaser*

A CIP record for this book is available from the British Library

ISBN 978–0–571–33102–4

2 4 6 8 10 9 7 5 3

Author's Note

The play takes place in Paris, London, Vichy and Colombey-les-Deux-Eglises, between 1913 and 1945.

The scenic design should be imaginative and highly mobile, so that changes of scene can be accomplished or suggested swiftly and unobtrusively, sometimes by light alone. The action of the play should never be held up by scene changes. Projections of still photographs or actuality footage could be a plus if affordable and practical. Captions, stating the location and year of key scenes, might be useful although not considered necessary in the original production.

The setting should include either a backcloth or a scrim/frontcloth that is a huge map of France. The map should include named places of the countries that surround her, namely Belgium, Luxembourg, Germany, Switzerland, Italy, Spain and England. The following places should also be named: Paris, Vichy, London, Verdun, Lyon, the Forest of Ardennes, Metz, Dunquerque, Boulogne, Compiègne, Colombey-les-Deux-Eglises, the Forest of Ardennes, the Maginot Line and the Rivers Somme, Marne, Meuse and Seine. The frontier between occupied France and unoccupied France (1940–42) should also be shown.

Pétain and de Gaulle play no other roles. All other parts can be played by four or more actors – the more the better, of course. Possible doubling is suggested on page 111.

This is essentially a true story. However, like most writers of history plays, I have sometimes blended several real people into one supporting character, I have imagined and invented almost all of the scenes and I have made guesses about what these people were really like in private.

I am greatly indebted to Admiral Philippe de Gaulle for giving me his permission to quote from his father's writings, including the *War Memoirs* and *Le Fil de l'épée* (*The Edge of the Sword*). Pétain's words are occasionally quoted in the play, as are some witnesses at the trial. I also owe a debt of gratitude to numerous historians and biographers among whom are J. R. Tournoux, Paul Webster, Charles Williams, Bernard Leftwidge, Brian Crozier, Malcolm Brown and Jean Lacouture.

J.L.

The **Patriotic Traitor** was first performed at Park Theatre, London, on 17 February 2016, produced by Bob Benton and Daniel Brodie for DB Productions in association with Park Theatre. The cast, in alphabetical order, was as follows:

Canon Pottevin, Cadet, Deladier, POW Officer, Léon Blum, Laval Niall Ashdown

Cadet, General le Gallet, POW Officer, Payen, De Courcel, Pomaret James Chalmers

Philippe Pétain Tom Conti

Charles de Gaulle Laurence Fox

Yvonne de Gaulle Ruth Gibson

General Joffre, General Herring, General Weygand, Lord Halifax Tom Mannion

Writer and Director Jonathan Lynn
Designer Georgia Lowe
Lighting Designer Mark Howland
Sound Designer Andrea J. Cox
Costume Supervisor Jackie Orton
Assistant Director Martha Geelan

Characters

THE PATRIOTIC TRAITOR

Act One

Sound: morbid drumbeats.
A ceiling fan slowly revolves.
The First Chamber of the Court of Appeal, July 1945.
High windows, shafts of light, window patterns on the
floor. Four square columns with Louis Quinze capitals –
optional.

Clerk Bring in the accused.

Marshal Pétain enters. He is frail, composed, with a
little white hair and a walrus moustache. He stands
erect. He is eighty-nine years old. The room falls
silent.
He wears his khaki uniform, with just one medal:
the Médaille Militaire. In his right hand he carries his
kepi with its triple wreath of golden oak leaves on a
black ribbon with a red ground. In his left hand, a pair
of gloves and a roll of white paper. Seven stars glitter
on his sleeve.
He strides forward. Majestically, he salutes. He sits.
Photographers surge forward, and take flash
photographs.

Accused, stand up.

Pétain stands. The photographers fall back.

What is your surname, Christian name, age and position?

Pétain Pétain, Philippe. Eighty-nine. Marshal of France.

We hear or see the Judge. Pétain faces out front.

Judge You are charged with treason, and with
collaborating with the enemy. Have you anything to say?

Pétain A Marshal of France does not ask anyone for mercy. Your judgement will have to face God's judgement. And that of posterity. That will suffice for my conscience and memory. I leave it to France.

Lights cross-fade to –
Pétain's bedroom/cell.
Lights: shadows of the window bars on the floor.
Pétain sits alone on the bed, mopping his brow. He fans himself with a document. It is sweltering.
Sound: thunder. A key turns a lock.
A Guard enters.

Pétain I want to see a priest.

Guard The chaplain's outside.

Pétain (*correcting him*) Sir!

Guard Sir.

He ushers in Canon Pottevin. The Guard exits.

Pottevin You wanted to see me, sir? Canon Pottevin, at your service.

Pétain I have things to say.

Pottevin Confession?

Pétain No – I just need somebody to talk to.

Pottevin nods and sits in the chair, which he moves from the centre. He is in awe of Pétain. He waits. He mops his sweating brow. There is a rumble of thunder.

Pottevin It's rather humid.

Pétain takes no notice.

Maybe there'll be a storm at last.

No response.

Shall we pray for God's forgiveness?

Pétain You can, if you like. Not me. It's de Gaulle's forgiveness I need. He is full of hatred, he's a man whose heart can't be touched. Do you think I'll be shot?

Pottevin stays silent. He doesn't know.

I sacrificed myself to France but France doesn't seem to appreciate it. (*Emotional.*) My power was legal, you know. I didn't seize it. They came to me and offered it. You think de Gaulle will shoot me?

Pottevin Doesn't that depend on the jury's verdict?

Pétain It depends on de Gaulle.

He stands.

And you know what? I made him! I gave him his big opportunity. (*Indicating the tiny bedroom.*) You see how he thanks me?

We hear strange music – Pétain appears lucid, but he is confusing the past and the present.

An ambitious fellow. Pride will destroy him . . . mark my words, pride will destroy him.

He turns.

This young man has done very well. A first-rate officer. I thought very highly of him. But he lacks experience of government, he has a great deal to learn, a great deal. He wants to govern without my advice – it's a mistake.

He recovers his senses.

Pride was always his problem . . . from the first day he joined my regiment. It was the eve of the Great War. France has suffered many calamities in her history, but the Great War was the worst of all . . . (*Testy.*) Of course, that's something else he disagrees with me about!

Lights up. A parade ground.

Lights: green shadows of tree branches. A sunny day. The bed and chair remain stage left.

Sound effects: troops marching. A distant marching band plays the 'Soldiers' Chorus' from Gounod's Faust.

De Gaulle enters and strolls across the parade ground, his nose in a book and two or three other books under his arm. He is in his early twenties, slim and studious.

Simultaneously Pétain sheds thirty years. He stands. He is fifty-nine years old.

Pétain Lieutenant?

De Gaulle stops, turns and sees Pétain.

It is customary to salute your commanding officer, or hadn't you heard?

De Gaulle Sorry, sir.

Pétain What's your name?

De Gaulle De Gaulle, sir.

Pétain takes the book from him, slightly curious.

Pétain What's the book?

De Gaulle Poetry, sir.

Pétain Poetry?

De Gaulle Yes. Oscar Wilde. An Irish poet, sir.

Pétain is surprised, and not particularly impressed.

Pétain Irish poet?

De Gaulle Yes, sir. I'm interested in poetry, sir. And my maternal ancestors were Irish.

Pétain And what does this Irish poet have to say?

De Gaulle I've been rather struck by something I just read. 'Each man kills the thing he loves.'

Pétain (*prosaically*) Well, that's not your job, Lieutenant. Your job is to kill the enemy – the Bosches, more than likely.

De Gaulle (*stiffly*) I appreciate that, sir.

Pétain And what are those other books?

De Gaulle Thucydides the Greek historian and Nietzsche. The German philosopher.

Pétain Bit of an intellectual, are you?

De Gaulle Yes, sir.

Pétain A little learning is a dangerous thing, you know.

De Gaulle I would agree with that, sir. But as I have a lot of learning, it is no problem in my case.

Pétain I see.

Amused, Pétain turns to go.

De Gaulle Colonel, may I just say that . . . I don't care what anyone says, I'm proud to be in your regiment.

Pétain (*turns back*) Are you being impertinent?

De Gaulle (*surprised*) No, sir. Certainly not, sir.

Pétain surveys him.

Pétain How old are you, de Gaulle?

De Gaulle Twenty-three, sir.

Pétain And do you hope to be a success in the army?

De Gaulle Yes, sir. I hope to be a general and commander-in-chief.

Pétain Is that all?

De Gaulle Sir?

Pétain I was joking.

De Gaulle (*uncomprehending*) Ah.

Pétain De Gaulle . . . have you no sense of humour?

De Gaulle No, sir. It seems to worry other people but it doesn't bother me.

Pétain sits on a bench or a wall.

Pétain Tell me, why did you ask to be posted here?

De Gaulle Because of you, sir, your belief in heavy artillery.

Pétain The General Staff don't share my belief.

De Gaulle (*with confidence*) I know, but we both know they're wrong.

Pétain A word of advice, sonny. If you're so ambitious, you'd better be less honest.

De Gaulle Not possible, sir. Honour for a man is like virtue for a woman: once lost, it is never regained.

Pétain is finding de Gaulle amusing.

Pétain You disapprove of women of easy virtue?

De Gaulle Naturally, sir.

Pétain That's not natural, that's bloody unnatural.

De Gaulle (*stiffly*) I'm sure you know best, sir.

Pétain (*chuckles*) Young man, I love three things in life – my country, the infantry and women.

De Gaulle Indeed, sir.

Pétain De Gaulle, why are you so . . . so serious?

De Gaulle War is inevitable. I am only twenty-three years old. And I have had a dream that on Thursday, August 15th 1914 I shall be killed in action.

Pétain You frightened?

De Gaulle (*hesitates momentarily*) Yes, sir. But God will give me courage. I know that I shall do my duty. So we shall see whether God gambles my life away or wishes to save me for some higher purpose.

Pétain I'm sure He'll realise that He needs you.

De Gaulle does not get the intended irony.

De Gaulle Perhaps. (*With intellectual excitement.*) But that depends on whether my dream was a message from my subconscious mind, a projection of my fears, as Sigmund Freud suggests. On the other hand, it might have been proof of the special theory of relativity which suggests that space and time are interwoven into a single continuum known as space-time.

Pétain is bewildered.

Pétain Single what?

De Gaulle According to Albert Einstein, past present and future are only illusions - very persistent ones. The future has happened – it exists so we're currently dead, in fact, in that case.

Petain What the hell are you talking about! Albert who? Who are these people?

De Gaulle German Jewish philosophers, sir.

Pétain Good God! Germans? And *Jews*? Listen to me. Soldiers are paid to fight, not to think. If you persist in thinking, you won't be very popular in the army.

Pétain turns to the audience. An Erik Satie piano piece is heard as we lose the exterior lighting.

Half a lifetime of friendship.

De Gaulle (*to the audience*) Half a lifetime. He was like a father to me.

He looks at Pétain.

Pétain He was like the son I never had. (*Chuckles.*) We were poles apart – he was a dreamer, a poet, an incurable romantic . . . people found him ridiculous.

De Gaulle He used to find me ridiculous. I don't know why, but some people did. He thought I took myself too seriously.

Pétain He took himself so seriously. But he took me seriously too. In 1913 I – alone – could see what was about to happen. They wouldn't listen. They wouldn't give me a proper job. Instead, I was teaching, of all things, at Saint-Cyr Military Academy.

Lights up. A Lecture Room.
A blackboard with three rules written on it:

GUNFIRE KILLS.

DEFENSIVE MANOEUVRES ARE NOT DISHONOURABLE.

NEVER LAUNCH AN ATTACK BEFORE THE ENEMY
IS WORN OUT.

De Gaulle sits among the audience, as do two Officer Cadets. Music fades.

Pétain Gentlemen, I believe in heavy artillery, not the all-out offensive.

First Cadet Sir, this goes against everything we've been taught. Surely it's necessary to take the offensive at all cost.

Pétain At all cost? You mean, risk losing?

First Cadet Isn't it essential for us to take the initiative?

Pétain What's wrong with letting the enemy take the initiative?

Second Cadet Sir . . . Colonel Grandmaison says that, in an offensive, rashness is the safest policy.

Pétain I wouldn't like to serve under him.

Second Cadet Colonel Bouvard argues that it's dangerous to let the enemy take the initiative. Regardless of heavy casualties, we must attack and break the enemy's will.

First Cadet That makes us the master, not the slave.

Second Cadet The Germans believe this.

Pétain They have more men. Perhaps they can afford this belief. We can't. Look carefully at my three Laws of Battle.

They are written up on the blackboard.

Pétain First Law: 'Gunfire Kills.' Heavy guns are the foundation of every operation. Then – and only then – charge the enemy with bayonets.

First Cadet But what if the Germans launch an offensive at all costs and break through our lines?

Pétain Would it really matter? What's the sense in never surrendering an inch of ground? Isn't it common sense to abandon a position if its defence is too costly?

De Gaulle stands up.

De Gaulle Well, obviously it is. Look at it this way . . .

Pétain Thank you, de Gaulle.

De Gaulle I was just agreeing with you, sir.

Pétain De Gaulle, your support is gratifying, but may I give this lecture please?

De Gaulle (*generously*) Certainly, sir.

He sits.

First Cadet Colonel, it may be common sense to surrender ground. But is it honourable?

De Gaulle is unable to keep silent and he stands up again.

De Gaulle The idea is to win!

Pétain (*sharp*) Thank you, de Gaulle!

De Gaulle I was just trying to help you explain –

Pétain *Silence!*

De Gaulle Yessir!

He sits, with great reluctance.

Pétain Now listen carefully. The second Law of Battle is: 'Defensive manoeuvres are not dishonourable.' They are *necessary.*

Pause.

Any questions on that?

De Gaulle manages to restrain himself.

And my third Law of Battle: 'Never launch an attack before the enemy is worn out.'

Pétain leaves. Lights fade, and only the three written rules remain lit.
A montage of sound effects: cheering crowds, steam engines leaving a station, and a band playing the Marseillaise.

Lights up. An operations room.
Night. A Corporal approaches Pétain, arriving.

Corporal Colonel Pétain?

Pétain *Brigadier* Pétain.

Corporal Sorry, Brigadier. General Joffre and General le Gallet will see you now.

Pétain Thank you.

He follows the Corporal into the operations room.

Corporal (*announcing him*) Brigadier Pétain.

Pétain Well done, lad.

General Joffre turns to him.

Joffre Ah, Pétain, we want your brigade to attack at dawn.

Pétain Why?

Le Gallet Because we must get on to the offensive.

Pétain Why, sir?

Le Gallet Why?

Pétain Yes. Why?

Joffre We're fighting a war, Pétain.

Pétain I am aware of that, sir. But I hope you understand that I shall never abandon my doctrine.

Le Gallet And what doctrine is that, my good man?

Pétain Do not launch an attack before the enemy is worn out.

Le Gallet Fine. But in the meantime perhaps you will be good enough to obey orders. The Thirty-third will attack at dawn.

Pétain When are we getting machine guns?

Le Gallet Look, we've had a few made, to satisfy public opinion. But machine guns won't make much difference to anything, they spatter the ramparts of a fort, that's all.

Joffre And they break down.

Le Gallet And they exhaust a battalion's ammunition in ten minutes.

Joffre Quite.

Le Gallet Quite. Furthermore, you have *men*. Always remember my first Law of Battle: 'Bullets are blind, only bayonets have intelligence.'

Joffre Now, order all units into an immediate offensive, with colours flying and bugles sounding the charge.

Pétain stares at him, then exits.

That man is too eager to concede French territory. Don't trust him, never will.

Le Gallet Quite.

Joffre Quite.

Sound: the Erik Satie music returns.
Lights cross-fade from the operations room as Pétain returns to . . .

The cell.

Pétain (*to Pottevin*) And all that intelligence was cut down in its prime by blind bullets. Only one thing was more blind than the bullets: our High Command. War has always taken its toll. As soon as our sons grow up we send them to die.

Smoke.
Lights: clouds and/or rain projected.
Sound: we hear a distant bugle call.

Bugles sounded the charge. The Germans had machine guns. Our young officers, in their ceremonial uniforms, white gloves and plumes, stayed calm and allowed themselves to be killed where they stood. Courage is no match for a machine gun.

Pétain leaves the cell. Pottevin exits in a different direction.
Lights change: we are no longer on the battlefield.
Sound: heavy artillery fire is in the distance.

Pétain De Gaulle?

De Gaulle Sir?

Pétain Remember my nemesis at Staff College, General Grandmaison?

De Gaulle The one who believed that, in an offensive, rashness is the safest policy?

Pétain Yes. I'm afraid he died today, testing his theory.

De Gaulle I'm sorry, but hardly surprised.

Pétain The High Command is expecting the Bosches to attack the bridge at Dinant tomorrow. We must hold it.

De Gaulle You know what tomorrow is?

Pétain No?

De Gaulle Thursday, August the fifteenth.

> *Their eyes meet. Pétain nods. De Gaulle exits.*
> *Sound: another bugle call. A burst of loud machine-gun fire, followed this time by an explosion.*

Pétain De Gaulle was wounded. Surgeons operated on him. But the Germans were advancing and, determined to avoid capture, he got to Charleroi in the car of a local lawyer, then to Lyon on successive trains for injured French soldiers. There he underwent more surgery. Realising that if he stayed in Lyon he could be caught in a trap, he hired a car the day after his surgery and left the city, determined not to be captured. I was intensely proud of him. He gave me hope. He made me feel safe. In a funny way, we fathered each other. I felt somehow that one day he'd take care of *me*.

> *Pétain crosses into . . .*

> *The operations room.*
> *He looks at the map. De Gaulle enters, limping and with left hand bandaged.*

De Gaulle Reporting for duty, sir.

Pétain De Gaulle? Back already. I was told you were blown up by a mine.

De Gaulle Not completely, sir. I also received a bullet in the hand.

Pétain Painful?

De Gaulle Of course!

Pétain I've selected you to be my adjutant.

De Gaulle I'm grateful naturally, sir, that you selected me . . . but may I request the command of a company so that I can fight in the line?

Pétain But you're not fully recovered.

De Gaulle Indeed not, sir, but I don't like paperwork.

Pétain You're very good at it.

De Gaulle I know, sir, but frankly, I disapprove of the directives that come down to my desk from the High Command.

Pétain But why must you go straight back to the front?

De Gaulle I would rather receive these idiotic commands than be responsible for giving them.

Pétain considers this view.

Pétain Fair enough.

Sombre music begins softly.

De Gaulle (*turns to the audience*) He understood the value of strength of character. In those days.

Pétain (*to the audience*) De Gaulle had strength of character. In those days.

Canon Pottevin is in the cell. Pétain talks to him.

In February 1916 we were close to losing the war. Historically our *philosophie* of defence has always depended upon a line of interconnected fortresses – Invulnerable, unbreakable fortresses. But between them there was always a fatal avenue –

Pottevin Through the town of Verdun?

Pétain Yes. Where the route from Metz to Paris crosses the River Meuse. Over the centuries Verdun has been subject to ten sieges. If the Kaiser could break through, he'd only be a day's march from Paris.

We hear the beginning of an incessant rumble of gunfire, that comes to dominate the action. Smoky clouds wash across upstage. Smoke is everywhere.
Music or dark instrumental sounds.
De Gaulle has gone. Pétain could be behind sandbags.

The bombardment of Fort Douaumont that began on February 21st 1916 was the heaviest in military history. It could be heard – clearly – a hundred miles away. They had Big Bertha, the biggest howitzer ever made by Krupp of Essen. Actually, nine Big Berthas. (*Surveying the scene.*) It was a firestorm. The air was sucked out of the world. A whirling tornado of flame and smoke flattened the pine trees and uprooted huge oaks, tossing them aside where they lay smouldering in the mud. Under orders, we continued a fruitless attempt to attack, over the top, over the top. But through the fog and the filth the men could see nothing. The gas and fierce heat burned their windpipes and lungs while the mud sucked panicking soldiers under as they struggled for dear life in a desperate and futile attempt not to be reduced to one more putrefying corpse – unrecognisable – one more unknown soldier – a pile of body parts, separated limbs and a torso built into the walls of the trenches.

A louder, nearer artillery barrage.

This horror lasted from February until July – five terrible months. We didn't have enough men, enough guns, we didn't even have enough barbed wire. Our losses were appalling. The army was completely disorganised and it buckled and the Commander-in-Chief, General Joffre, had nothing left to suggest. He summoned me.

> *Cross-fade to: the operations room.*
> *The artillery barrage continues.*
> *Pétain enters, meeting Generals Joffre and le Gallet.*
> *A young officer, Captain Deladier, now accompanies Pétain.*

Joffre Ah, Pétain . . .

Pétain General Joffre. This is my aide, Captain Deladier.

They salute.

Joffre It's not looking too good, Pétain.

Pétain No, sir. We're losing.

Le Gallet Stop this defeatist talk, sir.

Pétain I'm not a defeatist. I'm a realist. If we lose this battle we lose the war. We cannot continue sacrificing our men. We are running out.

Joffre We haven't got any more guns. Not as big as theirs.

Pétain What about air power?

Le Gallet Aeroplanes are for sport.

Pétain No, sir. They are bombing our positions with deadly accuracy.

Joffre Yes. (*Sighs.*) Pétain, I've . . . uh . . . decided . . . to put you in command of the army which we are forming to relieve Verdun.

Pétain Thank you, sir.

Joffre The Meuse must be held on the right bank. There can be no question of any other course than of checking the enemy, whatever the cost, on that bank.

Pétain I understand.

Joffre Good.

Pétain This is a last-ditch stand.

Joffre So what are you going to do?

Pétain Nothing.

Le Gallet Um – nothing?

Pétain An infantryman must never stick his head out of a hole too soon, or it'll be blown off. There's no chance of victory at the moment so I must simply avoid a defeat. I shall not move against the Germans until I have enough heavy guns and ammunition.

Le Gallet We must have a new offensive?

Pétain No, sir.

Le Gallet Then how do we win?

Pétain A counter-offensive, sir. You might have heard of it, it's a well-known military term.

Le Gallet Don't take that tone with me, Pétain.

Pétain We will not attack until we can win. Until then, we will hold the Germans where they are. We shall tell the army: they shall not pass.

Joffre Let's be practical. What do you need? Start with small arms. Grenades?

Le Gallet Five thousand?

Pétain Fifty thousand.

Le Gallet (*softly*) Good God!

The two Generals look at each other, and exit.

Pétain (*to Deladier*) Amateurs talk tactics. Professionals talk logistics.

Lights cross-fade to a single on Pétain. He turns to the audience as Deladier hands him a bottle of cognac, and exits.

I sent for de Gaulle. The night before he returned to the trenches, in a château away from the front lines, we had a conversation – the sort of conversation about 'life-and-death-and-what-they-mean' that people sometimes have the night before battle.

Lights up. The officers' mess.
De Gaulle sits in the chair, centre, reading. Pétain is fairly drunk. He pulls up another chair.

It was very confusing. Perhaps that was because I'd had a little too much cognac – though that wasn't the only reason I was confused. (*To de Gaulle.*) What are you reading nowadays?

He picks up two brandy goblets, hands one to de Gaulle.

De Gaulle Philosophy.

Pétain Who wrote it?

De Gaulle Nietzsche.

Pétain sits beside de Gaulle, intrigued. He pours a drink.

Pétain Who's that?

De Gaulle A German professor who lived in Switzerland. He went mad, and died about fifteen years ago.

Pétain Was he mad when he wrote his philosophy?

De Gaulle That's a matter of opinion – whether his madness caused his philosophy or his philosophy caused his madness.

Pétain You were reading him the day we met.

De Gaulle He fascinates me. He's not self-indulgent. He believes in Spartan discipline and the capacity to endure as well as inflict pain for important ends. He admires strength of will above all things.

Pétain So do I!

De Gaulle So do I!

Pétain (*finishes his drink*) Good. That's settled then. We like Nietzsche. Want some cognac?

> *De Gaulle holds out his glass. Pétain pours some into both their glasses.*

De Gaulle He wouldn't have liked you, though, sir.

Pétain Why the hell not?

De Gaulle He would not have been able to forgive your relatively humble origins. Look.

> *He shows the book to Pétain.*

'No morality is possible without good birth,' it says here.

Pétain (*drunkenly*) That's bloody ridiculous.

De Gaulle He also believes it's necessary to resist the democratic tendencies of the age.

Pétain Well, that's obvious.

De Gaulle Quite.

Pétain Quite.

De Gaulle He also says that women should be delicate, feminine and dainty, and that as soon as they achieve any independence they become intolerable.

Pétain (*drinking*) No question.

De Gaulle (*reads*) 'Man is trained for war and woman for the recreation of the warrior. All else is folly.'

Pétain What's the book? I'd like to read it.

De Gaulle *Thus Spake Zarathustra*. You wouldn't, you know.

Pétain Wouldn't I?

De Gaulle He sees no objection to the suffering of ordinary people if it is necessary in order to produce a great hero. He thinks the whole of the revolution from 1789 to 1815 is justified by Napoleon. The Revolution made Napoleon possible. We are right to desire the anarchic collapse of our entire civilisation if a Napoleon were to result.

Pétain Absolutely right.

De Gaulle Obviously. You can't haggle over greatness.

Pétain (*drunkenly*) Course you can't.

De Gaulle Course you can't.

Pétain (*pouring himself more cognac*) More?

De Gaulle Don't mind if I do.

Pétain pours it for him.

So you see, you do admire Nietzsche even though he wouldn't admire you.

Pétain I'm not so sure you're right about that – Napoleon came from humble origins too. I think that Nietzsche was a bit confused sometimes, that's all.

De Gaulle That's true. (*Drunkenly intrigued.*) How do you know, you sure you haven't read him?

Pétain Positive.

De Gaulle He regards compassion as a weakness to be resisted.

Pétain That's true for soldiers, isn't it?

De Gaulle I don't know. Is it?

Pétain I don't know. Is it?

De Gaulle Well – that's not what Christianity's about. That's the problem.

Pétain You're right!

He drinks.

De Gaulle And . . . you see . . . (*He sighs a deep sigh.*) Nietzsche's view of life is ultimately empty. But it's a temptation, when I feel melancholy, like tonight, that's what it is.

Pétain Is it?

De Gaulle Yes.

Pétain Do you?

De Gaulle Yes. Do I what?

Pétain What?

De Gaulle What?

Pétain Feel melancholy.

De Gaulle You too?

Pétain eyes him, trying to focus.

Pétain I think I'm losing track of this discussion.

De Gaulle No, what I'm saying is, when I'm reading Nietzsche I'm like a rabbit with a snake. Mesmerised, appalled, frightened and yet . . . attracted.

Pétain Like me with a whore.

De Gaulle Well . . . yes, in a way. But you see the flaw?

Pétain Yes. It's moving, like the rest of the room.

De Gaulle Not the floor. The flaw. In the . . .

Pétain Ointment.

De Gaulle Argument.

Pétain No. Tell me.

De Gaulle He doesn't believe in God.

Pétain Nor do I.

De Gaulle He says Christianity is the most fatal and seductive lie there ever was. 'No man of power has ever resembled the Christian ideal.' (*Anguished.*) And that's true. But what about compassion and humility, and love?

Pétain (*confused*) What about them?

De Gaulle Who will lead us with virtue? Are virtue and leadership incompatible?

Pétain Martyrs? Saints?

De Gaulle I don't know what to think, sir. What do you think?

Pétain (*firmly*) I think it's a mistake to read philosophy! I was perfectly clear on what I thought till we started this conversation.

He gets up, uncertainly.

De Gaulle You going?

Pétain There's a tart coming to my room. This warrior's going to have a little recreation. Goodnight.

Goes halfway off, stops and returns a few steps.

Good luck at dawn, my friend.

De Gaulle Thank you. But God will protect me.

Pétain eyes him with amusement and affection, then totters out.

Lights up. Pétain's cell.
He sits on his bed. In his head he hears – and we hear –
Music/additional sound: a shell whistles overhead and explodes. The rumbling of artillery continues unabated.

Soldiers (*pre-recorded*) Bullets are blind. Bayonets have intelligence. Bullets are blind. Bayonets have intelligence, Bullets are blind . . .

A burst of machine-gun fire. Silence.
Then distant artillery gunfire continues under . . .

Pétain In six days of bitter fighting defending Fort Douaumont, de Gaulle's company was wiped out. He was missing in action. I wrote the citation with a heavy heart. (*Stands up.*) 'Captain de Gaulle, company commander, known for his high intelligence and moral courage, when his company was undergoing devastating bombardment with the enemy attacking from all sides, led his men into a furious assault and fierce hand-to-hand fighting, the only solution he deemed compatible with his sense of military honour. He fell in the fray. An outstanding officer in every respect.' And I conferred on him the Cross of the Legion of Honour – posthumously. Then it turned out he wasn't dead. Fucking typical!

Lights up. A POW camp.
Barbed-wire shadows, on the floor and maybe on the back wall. A searchlight flashes past, if possible.

The sound of the artillery has gone.
De Gaulle sits apart from the others. He is heavily bandaged. A crutch lies beside him. He is writing, thinking, pencil and paper in hand. First Officer lies on a straw mattress. Second Officer plays with a football.

First Officer Who are you writing to?

De Gaulle Nobody.

First Officer I'm writing to my sweetheart.

De Gaulle (*politely*) Indeed.

First Officer What are you writing?

De Gaulle Notes for my first book. On the use of tanks and armoured divisions.

First Officer (*amused*) First book? There'll be others, will there?

De Gaulle Of course.

He continues writing. The First Officer is sympathetic.

First Officer No one to write to, then?

De Gaulle is trying to be patient, although he dislikes interruptions.

De Gaulle My parents. I write to them regularly.

First Officer No wife?

De Gaulle No.

First Officer What about a girlfriend?

De Gaulle What about minding your own business?

Irritated, he puts down his pencil and paper, and tidies up his newspaper.

First Officer Where did you get a French newspaper?

De Gaulle Actually it's not French, it's *Die Frankfurter Zeitung*.

Second Officer I don't hold with reading enemy newspapers.

De Gaulle Then it's fortunate that you're not capable of doing so. How else do you find out what the enemy's thinking?

Second Officer Who cares? For me the war is over.

De Gaulle stares at him coldly.

De Gaulle Not for me.

He gets up and starts pulling on some old clothes.

First Officer He's going to try to escape again.

De Gaulle turns, dressed as an old peasant woman. He is thoroughly unconvincing.

De Gaulle How do I look?

They laugh.

Second Officer You're so bloody useless at escaping.

De Gaulle I'm good at it. I've got out of the camp five times. I've just been unlucky that they always find me.

Second Officer Unlucky?

The Officers laugh. De Gaulle is not amused.

De Gaulle At least I try.

First Officer What would Pétain think of all your dressing up?

De Gaulle He would approve. He can think laterally. He's risen through the ranks through sheer ability. He obeys orders, but he's proud and can't be pressured. This pride protects him and gives him prestige. He's the ideal commander.

Second Officer The way you describe Pétain . . . that's how you see yourself too, isn't it?

De Gaulle Yes. I say it in all humility.

Second Officer Oh, I didn't notice the humility.

The Officers smile. De Gaulle does not, but he is not perturbed.

De Gaulle Was that a joke?

Second Officer (*defiantly*) Yes.

De Gaulle (*pleased*) Good, good.

Pause.

You know, we are going to win this war at last.

First Officer You hope.

De Gaulle I know. Instead of killing all our men, Pétain's using the new victory weapon – the tank. And waiting for the Americans to arrive.

Second Officer Well, thank God we're winning – but I'm glad I'm out of it.

De Gaulle How can you be glad?

Second Officer I'm not a professional soldier – I don't like war.

De Gaulle You think I do?

First Officer You don't ever seem frightened.

De Gaulle No.

Second Officer Doesn't your life matter to you?

De Gaulle Yes. But then I look at the stars . . .

He looks up.

Second Officer (*puzzled*) So?

De Gaulle They confirm the insignificance of things.

First Officer Are you trying to tell us that you consider yourself insignificant?

De Gaulle Compared to the universe, yes. Not compared to you, of course.

Lights fade to: spotlight on Pétain.

Pétain (*to the audience*) Everything he said about himself was true. And about me. (*His eyes twinkle.*) I too say it in all humility.

As the lights cross-fade, Deladier enters the courtroom, having exchanged his uniform jacket for a civilian jacket. He has aged thirty years. He sits. Pétain watches.
Fernand Payen, for the defence, stands. The Dean of the French Bar, he's seventy-three years old, thin reedy voice, apparently hanging on to life by a thread.

Payen Monsieur Deladier, you were the Prime Minister in 1940.

Deladier I was one of the Prime Ministers in that year, yes.

Payen Do you think that the Marshal betrayed his country?

Deladier (*carefully*) In all conscience I must reply that, in my opinion, yes.

Pétain Good God!

Deladier Marshal Pétain betrayed the duties of his office.

Payen Have you anything to say, Marshal Pétain?

Pétain I will not answer any questions that are put to me.

And Pétain stalks back to –

The cell.
And sits on the bed.

Deladier's a disloyal bastard. And he's got a bloody nerve. He's the man who went to Munich. He gave the Führer the go-ahead. But I saved France. Not once, not twice – three times! Verdun was the first. Seven hundred thousand men died in that hell. Worse even than Stalingrad. But it was the turning point. And I won the respect of the Germans. They called me 'der alter Fuchs' – the old fox. 'Ich bin ein alter Fuchs.'

Pétain wipes his eyes. He's almost crying with bitterness and anger.

No wonder I was bitter. When I had nearly won they made Nivelle Commander-in-Chief. Nivelle, the military genius who recaptured Fort Douaumont on the twenty-fourth of October at the cost of one hundred thousand lives. *One* fortress. He was a self-confident publicity-seeking windbag. So, inevitably, in 1917 the army mutinied. And I saved France a second time.

Soldiers start singing the Internationale. (This might be the cast, live, or sound effect. Depends on the size of the cast.)
Lights up, as Pétain crosses to –

The battlefield.
Distant gunfire. Heavy artillery. And smoke . . .

Soldiers
'So comrades, come rally,
And the last fight let us face,
The Internationale unites the human race.'

As Pétain arrives, accompanied by Captain Deladier,
they boo and jeer. (Depending on the theatre or the
size of the cast, they might be at the back of the
auditorium.) He stands on something, waits, then
speaks to the crowd.

Pétain I want to talk to you, man to man. Yes, you have
reason to complain. This war is too long and too hard.
You need good food. You need rest. But this war has
been imposed on us, and we must win it. I guarantee
that I shall not send you into battle unless you are well
covered by artillery. No more suicidal attacks. You can't
fight against guns with men. We shall not attack until we
have enough guns and ammunition. I care about your
lives, more than my own. (*His voice rises.*) But remember
your wives and children, your parents, your land . . . It
would be slavery under the Germans. Be patient, be
strong, believe in France, and draw strength from her like
the strength of those who believe in God.

The Soldiers cheer, and disperse.

Deladier General?

Pétain What is it, Deladier?

Deladier We have forty shirkers. Men with self-inflicted
hand wounds.

Pétain Shoot them.

Deladier I'm sorry, did you say shoot them, sir?

Pétain Yes, I will not have cowardice in my army.

Deladier does not move.

On second thoughts, have them bound and thrown from
the other side of the parapet to the trenches nearest the
enemy. They will spend the night there . . .

Deladier Will they be left there, to starve?

Pétain Are you questioning my orders, Captain?

Deladier No, sir. It's just that . . . just now, you seemed so sympathetic to the men.

Pétain You catch more flies with honey than with vinegar.

He turns to the audience.

Not too much compassion there, I'm afraid. Well, we couldn't afford it. (*His eyes twinkle.*) But Nietzsche would have approved, don't you think?

Sounds: crowds cheering, bells ringing, The Marseillaise . . . The war is over.

Lights up. A smart café.
 Music: a palm court trio, playing romantic music. (With a large cast, couples may be dancing in the shadows.)
 Yvonne Vendroux is sitting at a table, sipping coffee. She is a confident young woman. There are two extra cups and a coffee pot on the table.
 De Gaulle and a young Captain enter. They approach Yvonne's table.

Captain Good evening, Yvonne.

Yvonne Good evening.

They kiss on both cheeks.

Captain Allow me to introduce an army friend of mine – Charles de Gaulle. Charles, this is Yvonne Vendroux, my cousin.

De Gaulle Good evening.

Yvonne Good evening, sir.

He shakes hands with her. It nearly breaks her arm.

Captain See you later.

De Gaulle Wait! Don't leave.

Captain *Courage.*

The Captain exits. De Gaulle is uncertain what to do next.

Yvonne Would you like to sit down?

De Gaulle Thank you.

De Gaulle sits at the dainty little table. He is much too big, and balances precariously, stiff and awkward. There's a pause.

Yvonne So, Monsieur de Gaulle . . .

De Gaulle Captain de Gaulle.

Yvonne I'm sorry. Captain.

De Gaulle Oh. Please don't apologise. I shouldn't have corrected you. *I* apologise.

A pause.

Yvonne Coffee?

De Gaulle Thank you.

There's an embarrassing silence while she pours.

Yvonne I gather you are a professional soldier.

De Gaulle I am.

Yvonne You enjoy fighting?

De Gaulle It is my duty.

Yvonne Quite. But . . . were you frightened?

De Gaulle Yes. At first. But I didn't show it, I'm glad to say. I trusted in God. And then, after I was injured I never lacked courage again. And I never shall.

Yvonne Never?

De Gaulle I expected to be killed, you see. A premonition, a dream. Since then, I feel that my life is no longer my own – it belongs to a destiny as yet undiscovered.

Yvonne (*a small smile*) Isn't that just a little self-important?

De Gaulle Is it? Sorry.

Yvonne No, don't apologise.

De Gaulle Sorry. I mean, sorry, I didn't mean to say sorry. I seem to be a little nervous today.

Yvonne (*mischievously*) It is a little strange for someone who never lacks courage to be so nervous.

De Gaulle All I meant was I'll never again lack courage *in war*.

Yvonne Do you like war?

De Gaulle How could anyone like it?

Yvonne You chose it as your life's work.

De Gaulle I chose to serve France, and to defend her if necessary. But war is brutal, and futile. Between the French and the Germans alternate victories have settled nothing. Sometimes, worn out by war, the two peoples seem to come close together, but they are like two panting wrestlers leaning on each other only to catch breath.

Yvonne eyes him with amusement and interest.

Yvonne Do you always talk in this fashion?

De Gaulle What fashion?

Yvonne I suppose that answers my question.

De Gaulle looks inquiringly at her.

That was a little joke.

De Gaulle (*pleased*) Ah.

Yvonne You sounded as though you were addressing a public meeting.

De Gaulle I would apologise, but I hardly dare.

Yvonne Thank goodness. Of what are you so nervous? Women?

De Gaulle shakes his head.

De Gaulle Just you.

Yvonne Me? What do you know about me?

De Gaulle Everything. You went to a convent school, your father makes biscuits, you have come to Paris for New Year's Eve . . .

Yvonne Why should any of that make you nervous?

De Gaulle What makes me nervous is your dignity, your repose, the honesty that shines out of your eyes.

Yvonne Are you trying to tell me – (*with hope*) that I'm beautiful?

De Gaulle Well, I – uh – I can't honestly . . . I'm not much of an expert on . . . Striking, perhaps might be the word.

Yvonne (*acid*) Thank you.

De Gaulle Sorry, I must be honest . . . Shall we dance?

Yvonne No.

De Gaulle Please. I find you most . . . attractive.

Unenthusiastically, she agrees. As they dance, lights cross-fade to a spotlight on Pétain, watching.

Pétain (*to the audience*) In 1921 they were married. And so, by chance, was I. Well, I was sixty-six, I'd sown my wild oats, I decided it was about time to settle down. He went off to Staff College – and as always he was in trouble pretty soon.

Lights up. Pétain's office, Army GHQ.
Pétain is now sitting behind a splendid desk in his office in the Boulevard des Invalides.
De Gaulle enters. Pétain rises from his desk and crosses the room to meet him. They shake hands.

So. How's married life treating you, de Gaulle?

De Gaulle Fine, thank you, sir. Yvonne's expecting a baby boy.

Pétain When?

De Gaulle December.

Pétain (*knowingly*) Aye, aye. (*Starts counting up to nine on his fingers.*) February, March, April, May . . . oh yes, that's all right.

De Gaulle (*stiffly*) It certainly is.

Pétain Baby boy, did you say? How do you know?

De Gaulle God will give me a son. And I would like to name him Philippe.

Pétain After me?

De Gaulle If I may.

Pétain Of course you may. I'm honoured.

De Gaulle Will you be the godfather?

Pétain I'll go to church for that. Thank you.

De Gaulle And how are *you* finding married life, sir? Managing all right, are you?

Pétain Why not?

De Gaulle Well . . . at your age, I mean . . .

Pétain is staring coldly at him.

Sorry, sir.

Having silenced de Gaulle, Pétain consults some papers on his desk, and sits.

Pétain You've been in trouble at Staff College, de Gaulle.

De Gaulle I believe I have.

Pétain I have the confidential report on you here. I'm not supposed to tell you what it says.

De Gaulle Of course you're not.

Pétain Would you like me to read it to you?

De Gaulle Yes, please.

Pétain Sit down. (*Reading.*) 'An intelligent, knowledgeable and conscientious officer. Full of character. Brilliant and talented.'

De Gaulle (*judiciously*) I think I would agree with that.

Pétain 'Unfortunately he mars these indisputable qualities by his excessive self-confidence, unwillingness to listen to the opinions of others, and his attitude of a "king in exile".'

De Gaulle Colonel Moyrand actually means that I was not willing to listen to him.

Pétain Why not?

De Gaulle He's a fool.

Pétain You think he's a fool because he always disagrees with you?

De Gaulle No, I don't mind people disagreeing with me *per se* – but it *is* an indication of stupidity, obviously.

Pétain gives him a look, then continues reading.

Pétain 'De Gaulle was in command of the Army Corps during the first period of the manoeuvres: showed decision, calm and powers of command.'

Pétain looks up at de Gaulle.

De Gaulle Perhaps he's not always wrong.

Pétain 'But he also showed a lack of balanced judgement, adopted solutions somewhat unsuited to the situation, as he frankly acknowledged.'

De Gaulle I made no such acknowledgement. Can you imagine?

Pétain No, I must say I can't. (*Reads on.*) 'He mixed little with the other officers and almost always arrived at the lecture hall by himself.'

De Gaulle That is true. I make no apology for it.

Pétain (*puts down the report*) What's the real cause of all this trouble?

De Gaulle The next war, whenever it comes, won't be about trench warfare. But all the lecturers spent years in the trenches and they can't think any other way. I don't mean that we should ignore all the lessons of history, but for me the future will involve the study and application of principles from physics such as mass, speed, points of pressure, levers . . . and we have been kept on the sterile chemistry of trench warfare.

Pétain And were there free discussions?

De Gaulle Yes. And I said what I thought, with great frankness.

Pétain I can imagine.

Pétain gets up and crosses away.

De Gaulle Will I get a lectureship at Staff College?

Pétain De Gaulle, as you know, you can pass out of college in one of three classifications: Very Good, Good, or Adequate. Do you know what category you've been placed in?

De Gaulle 'Very Good', obviously.

Pétain 'Adequate'.

De Gaulle 'Adequate'? Is that a joke?

Pétain A joke?

De Gaulle I don't have a very acute sense of humour, you know, so if it's a joke . . .

Pétain No, it's not a joke, it's a fact.

De Gaulle I can't believe it.

Pétain I have no love for Staff College. They nearly finished me off as well. I have seen to it that you pass out 'Good'.

De Gaulle No, you mean 'Very Good'.

Pétain No. 'Good'.

De Gaulle (*stands up again*) That doesn't satisfy me.

Pétain It doesn't satisfy me either. But it's the best I can do.

De Gaulle That means I won't get a lectureship.

Pétain That's right. But there is a way back.

De Gaulle I shall never go back to that miserable dump until I'm the director of it.

Pétain Yes, well . . . for the moment you are not to be Director of Staff College. They have drafted you to Army Headquarters as a staff officer in the supplies and rations department. With a special responsibility.

De Gaulle For supplying tanks?

Pétain No – for food storage.

De Gaulle My God!

Pétain I'm sorry. Colonel Moyrand is rather short-sighted. It's his fault this has happened.

De Gaulle No, it's my fault. I never blame anyone else. To blame others is a sign of weakness.

Pétain I'll help you all I can. But at the moment there's nothing else I can do.

De Gaulle I understand.

Pétain Except . . .

Pétain leans forward, but he appears hesitant and tentative.

I have had an idea for a book. We could collaborate on it. It would be about the French soldier through the centuries. I envisage an important philosophic work, and it would finish on a very high note, showing how *I* overcame the crisis of morale in 1917.

De Gaulle I see. A *very* high note.

Pétain Are you trying to be funny, de Gaulle?

De Gaulle Certainly not, sir. What an idea!

Pétain Perhaps you would do some work on it for me? I'm not much of a writer.

De Gaulle I am a magnificent writer. I shall see that it is a masterpiece.

Pétain (*to the audience*) And so work was begun on my book.

De Gaulle (*to the audience*) And so I began work on my book.

As the set changes, lights cross-fade. De Gaulle exits.

Pétain And I came up with an original idea, to rescue de Gaulle's career. I summoned the head of Staff College.

Enter General Hering, at a smart pace. He stands at attention while Pétain berates him. Upstage, de Gaulle, with Yvonne's help, changes into a ceremonial uniform.

Pétain General Hering, the whole affair is a monstrous miscarriage of justice. De Gaulle's grading is a scandal and he's obviously the best young officer you've had for years. You are going to arrange a series of lectures to be given to the entire school – by de Gaulle.

Hering Are you serious?

Pétain I am. I want to teach those professors a lesson.

Hering salutes, and hurries away.

(*Chuckles.*) It was a calculated insult to the lot of them, being lectured by a Second Grade Captain. But they'd have to come because I'd be in the chair. The subject was 'The Qualities of Leadership'.

A huge tricolour flag flies in.
Several Generals sit upstage, De Gaulle comes downstage.

Pétain (*to the audience*) Gentlemen of the Staff College, Captain de Gaulle is about to tell you his ideas. I ask you to listen attentively.

De Gaulle places his sword on the table and takes off his white gloves.
He speaks to the audience without notes.

De Gaulle Leadership. Hannibal was simple and reserved. Caesar was shrewd and eloquent. Napoleon passionate, tormented and familiar. But they, and all great leaders, had one thing in common: prestige. A prestige that is carefully and psychologically created by making sure that they are impenetrable to their subordinates. Because they have mystery they seem superhuman to their armies and that is how they maintain morale, no matter what.

De Gaulle looks at Pétain.

True leaders are strong characters. But strong characters have a difficult path to the top. Selection boards prefer personal charm to merit. Those who are blunt and uncompromising are rarely loved and seldom looked upon with favour.

Pétain nods in full agreement.

Leaders are not only fighters, they are gamblers. A leader will pay his debts with his life. He does not shelter behind superiors, rely on textbooks, nor cover himself with bureaucratic reports. He confronts the situation. Great soldiers, in fact, have often disregarded orders, like Pélissier at Sebastopol who read the Emperor's telegrams *after* the battle.

The listening Generals react with distaste.

Nelson too: the First Lord of the Admiralty received Admiral Jellicoe's report after the Battle of Jutland and wrote with regret: 'He has all of Nelson's qualities except one – he does not know how to disobey.'

Europe is now stricken with a decadence that is destroying authority. The social, moral and political orders are in decline, but men need authority just as they need food and sleep. As the traditional foundations of authority are shaken, others appear based on the superior power of a few individuals. The masses today accord authority not to princes, but to those who can assert it. No prince has ever been obeyed like self-made dictators. The true commander relies on his real worth and his prestige, not his high rank, for obedience.

We seldom respect what we know too well. All religions have secret shrines. No man is a hero to his valet. The man of character, while carefully watching everybody else, will avoid revealing himself. He deliberately keeps secrets and preserves the element of surprise. The credulity of the masses will do the rest, believing the leader has mysterious powers peculiar to himself.

De Gaulle stops for a sip of water, which he pours from a carafe into a tumbler, and he freezes as –

Lights cross-fade to:

Pétain It was an impressive performance. I thought it very nice of him to say such things about me.

Hering You thought he was talking about you?

Hering exits.
Lights up –

De Gaulle's flat in Paris.
Domestic furniture.
Yvonne de Gaulle is cuddling a baby. A doorbell rings. Then a Maid (or Manservant) appears.

Maid Marshal Pétain is here.

Yvonne Show him in.

Maid Very good, madame.

Maid exits. After a moment Pétain enters, with flowers.

Yvonne Hello, Marshal. Welcome.

Pétain (*with warmth*) Ah, the new baby. Here, some flowers.

Yvonne Thank you. How beautiful.

Pétain What's her name again?

Yvonne Anne.

Pétain Anne. Of course. (*To baby.*) Hello, Anne. Goo goo goo.

Anguished screams from the baby.

Yvonne Sorry, it's just that she doesn't know you.

Pétain And I always thought I was attractive to girls.

Yvonne Generally, yes. But not this one.

Petain And how's little Philippe? And the – other one?

Yvonne Elizabeth. Very well, thank you.

She cuddles the baby. It stops crying.

Pétain Where's de Gaulle?

Yvonne Perhaps he doesn't know you're here. I'll go and tell him.

Yvonne exits, with the baby. Pétain makes himself comfortable in an armchair. De Gaulle enters.

De Gaulle Bonjour, Marshal.

Pétain Congratulations.

De Gaulle On what?

Pétain On the new baby.

De Gaulle If this is one of your jokes, it doesn't amuse me.

Pétain Jokes?

De Gaulle Surely you know? Yvonne was knocked down by a car six months ago, crossing the Boulevard des Invalides.

Pétain But she wasn't hurt. She looks fine.

De Gaulle But she was pregnant.

Pause.

The baby is not fine. The baby is not normal. I would give everything, everything, health, fortune, promotion, career, if only Anne were a little girl like all the others.

De Gaulle takes out a handkerchief and blows his nose loudly. He is deeply upset, but trying not to show it.

Pétain I'm sorry . . . I had no idea . . .

De Gaulle (*curt*) Understood. (*Puts his handkerchief away.*) Please sit down again. A glass of wine?

Pétain Thank you. (*Empathising with de Gaulle.*) Are you going to put her away somewhere?

De Gaulle gives him a look, then pours wine for all three of them.

De Gaulle We're thinking of going to live somewhere in the country. Where it's peaceful. We thought . . . it might be better for Anne and the others to grow up there.

Pétain But the army . . .

De Gaulle (*interrupting*) I am thinking of resigning my commission and giving up my military career.

Pétain (*astonished*) You can't be serious.

De Gaulle Well, it's not exactly a glittering success, is it?

Pétain doesn't know how to reply. Yvonne enters. De Gaulle hands a glass of wine to her as he speaks.

My lectures fell totally flat. They were brilliant, but now I am resented even more than I was before.

Pétain I can't deny you've had setbacks – but so did I, to start with. If war hadn't broken out in 1914 I'd have retired as a colonel, aged sixty, having achieved nothing.

De Gaulle And what have I achieved? You talk of 'setbacks'. I am thirty-seven years old. By the age of thirty Alexander of Macedonia had conquered half the ancient world; and Bonaparte had been a general for several years. And I am a captain. I have been frozen in the rank of captain for twelve years, since 1915. It is wholly appropriate that I should have been put in charge of refrigeration.

Pétain (*hopefully*) Was that a joke?

De Gaulle Absolutely not! I felt myself born to serve France, and to lead others in her service. But the years are passing, in obscurity and misunderstanding. And now . . . this. Marshal, I have been studying the story of Job. I have been thinking about Christ on the cross. Did he really think his Father had forsaken him? Job was being tested, Christ was being sacrificed. Am I being tested, am I being sacrificed? But why?

Pétain It occurs to me that it's not just you who is suffering. What about your wife? And your daughter, perhaps?

Yvonne Quite.

De Gaulle looks at her, then at his feet.

De Gaulle I'm ashamed. I'm sorry. You make me ashamed.

Yvonne goes to comfort him. He moves away from her, wipes his eyes, blows his nose and sits. He sits straight as a ramrod, as always.

I understand. I am not being tested, I'm not being sacrificed. How could I have had such delusions of grandeur? I'm being punished, that's what it is. I'm being punished for the sin of pride.

Yvonne For God's sake, Charles, you're still talking about you. Anne is the one who's suffering.

De Gaulle Perhaps she's not, she understands so little. But if she is, then we all are. We are all being punished for my vanity, my pride, my self-importance. (*Stands.*) I was wrong. I've been wrong all along. (*In real emotional pain.*) God is not on my side!

Yvonne (*gently*) God is on everyone's side.

Pétain Or nobody's.

De Gaulle What will I do now? Now that I'm humble?

Yvonne can't help smiling.

Yvonne Now that you're humble? I expect you'll do the same as you did before.

De Gaulle No. Everything will be different from now on. I'll see to that. I shall give up my career to care for our wounded child. And little Philippe, he needs me too.

Yvonne And what will we live on?

De Gaulle I'll find a job. I'm not totally without ability, even if the army thinks I am.

Yvonne I don't want you to find a job. You've got a job. You're a soldier.

De Gaulle But just a captain, after fourteen years.

Yvonne Isn't that enough, now that you're humble?

De Gaulle is aghast.

De Gaulle I'm doing it again! I'm sorry, it's just hard for me to come to terms with the fact that I'm not needed.

Yvonne (*to Pétain*) He will be needed, won't he?

Pétain Now is the time to be strong. You were strong before, many times, when others would have found it too hard and would have given up. Don't give up. Now is the moment that you need the faith that I have envied so often. Don't give up. I'll help you every way I can. Don't give up.

De Gaulle I don't want to seem ungrateful, Marshal, but with your help I have tried to attract attention and I have merely aroused hostility. I have no future in the army.

Pétain You have. It may not be the glittering future that you hoped for, but it will not be dishonourable.

De Gaulle It would be worse than dishonourable – it would be undistinguished!

Yvonne There you go again.

De Gaulle If I can't make a worthwhile contribution I'd rather leave.

Pétain Who knows what's worthwhile? Until you recover your faith in yourself, have faith in me. I shall see that you get your chance.

Yvonne is touched.

Yvonne Thank you, Marshal.

De Gaulle Thank you, sir.

Pétain You can trust me, de Gaulle.

De Gaulle I know. I know.

Pause.

I know.

Lights fade to –

Pétain's cell.
Pétain, crossing to his cell, sitting on his bed.
Pottevin is there to listen.

Pétain When I told him I'd see to it that he'd get his chance, the irony had not yet dawned on me: that his chance would come at my expense. I helped him, and in time he grew strong again.

Pottevin Did he eventually buy a house in Colombey?

Pétain Yes, but he didn't retire. Course not! A megalomaniac like him? Ha! And, finally, promotion came. Major in 1928, Lieutenant-Colonel in 1934 I think it was . . .

Pétain stands and struts self-importantly round the room.

And I was promoted in 1934. Joined the government. Minister of War. I was seventy-eight and fit as a fiddle. From then on I was in and out of government – they couldn't do without me, you see. They needed an elder statesman. (*Now he's talking to the audience.*) As for de Gaulle, all that stuff about having to disobey orders, he was beginning to apply it to himself. And then came that bloody business over my book. I went to visit him in Colombey.

Lights up.

De Gaulle's study. Outside, a garden.
  Window gobos: it's green and sunny outside.
  Pétain crosses to de Gaulle and shakes hands.

De Gaulle Welcome, sir.

Pétain So, how's . . . um . . . what's your wife's name?

De Gaulle Yvonne.

Pétain Yvonne, yes. (*His memory is failing.*) How is she?

De Gaulle Fine. You like my trees? Beautiful, aren't they?

Pétain They're all right. What are they?

De Gaulle Chestnuts.

Pétain's eyes light up like a small boy's.

Pétain Ah. Conkers! Did you ever have conker fights?

De Gaulle Of course. (*He sits.*) Seen the papers today?

Pétain I don't read the papers. Doom and gloom merchants, the lot of them.

De Gaulle We'll lose the war, you know, when it comes.

Pétain Nonsense. I'm still here, fit as a fiddle.

De Gaulle But we are totally unprotected.

Pétain Unprotected? We've got the Maginot Line. It's impregnable.

De Gaulle It's a delusion.

Pétain Don't be ridiculous. Use your eyes.

De Gaulle walks over to a wall map.

De Gaulle What about the Belgian frontier? There's no Maginot Line there.

Pétain The Forest of Ardennes is impenetrable. High bluffs, escarpments, narrow mountain paths. That's why they always try to come at us through Verdun. We've stopped them in Belgium before, we'll stop them again.

De Gaulle (*trying to be patient*) Times have changed. We no longer need a mass of inferior unskilled men. Modern warfare is about mobility, the lightning strike – the blitzkrieg. Look! There's a gaping hole between the Belgian forests and the sea. Paris is only one hundred and twenty miles from the border – six days' march, three hours in a tank, one hour in a plane. We lose one battle, it's over. Each time in the last century that Paris was taken, the resistance of the rest of France lasted less than an hour.

Pétain De Gaulle, you never learn. You lobby incessantly. You interfere in politics. You argue with your superiors. You mix with the Socialists. You never take no for an answer. And all you do is irritate people. No wonder you never get any advancement.

De Gaulle Haven't you just described your own career, till Verdun?

Pétain That's different. I was proved right.

De Gaulle I shall be too. I'm in despair, preaching in the wilderness. If we'd had an armoured corps when Hitler occupied the Rhineland we would have changed the course of history. We should have acted with surprise, ruthlessness and speed.

Pétain Nonsense. We learned all about offensives in 1916. The defensive is infinitely superior.

De Gaulle In 1916 it was. Not today. You're living in the past, sir, can't you see that?

Pétain Everyone's out of step except you, eh?

De Gaulle can't be bothered to reply.

I came here to discuss something much more important.

De Gaulle What could be more important than this?

Pétain My history of the French Army. My book.

De Gaulle You mean, my book?

Pétain Yes, I understand you intend to publish it under your own name.

De Gaulle (*cautiously*) That's right.

Pétain Hell's bells, de Gaulle, you were my staff writer. I merely asked for your assistance. It was my book.

De Gaulle But I wrote it. Every word.

Pétain You stole it.

There is an icy pause.

De Gaulle You insult me, sir.

Pétain is spluttering with rage.

Pétain It's a fact. You were a staff writer. You were privileged to be invited to work on my book. But it was mine! I was your commander.

De Gaulle That may be the military tradition, but it doesn't make it any less nonsensical. I wrote it.

Pétain It was all my idea.

De Gaulle I acknowledge that in the dedication.

He takes a piece of paper from his desk and tries to give it to Pétain. Pétain waves it away.

Pétain I know all about that. You sent it to me. It won't do.

De Gaulle What did it say?

Pétain I can't remember now.

De Gaulle I'll read it to you.

Pétain I don't want to hear it.

De Gaulle 'To Marshal Pétain, who wanted this book to be written, who directed with his advice the writing of the first five chapters, and thanks to whom the last are the history of our victory.'

Pétain I didn't want the book to be written as your book, I opposed that. I wanted it to be my book.

De Gaulle How could it have been when I wrote it?

Pétain We've been through all that. I don't want that dedication. I opposed this book.

De Gaulle But *I* want the dedication. I want to acknowledge you. Don't deprive me of this. You thought of it.

Pétain So you admit it. You admit that you stole it.

De Gaulle I didn't steal it. You thought of it, I wrote the bloody thing!

Pétain How dare you speak to me like that?

De Gaulle Look. What would you like it to say?

Pétain takes a piece of paper out of his pocket, and reads:

Pétain 'To Marshal Pétain – before whom I kneel in grateful homage.'

De Gaulle (*after a moment*) Sorry, sir. I can't do that.

Pétain Why not?

De Gaulle I have my pride.

Pétain We know all about your pride. It brought you your daughter, didn't it?

There is a tense pause. Pétain bites his lip.

De Gaulle How can you sink so low? To think I admired you once. Loved you, even.

Pétain You refuse my request?

De Gaulle Utterly.

Pétain Rules are rules. An officer from Staff College works for his chief anonymously.

He starts to go.

This is goodbye.

De Gaulle (*with sadness*) You're losing your sense of proportion.

Pétain (*exploding*) You turkey-cock! I shall have nothing more to do with you, ever.

De Gaulle I expect I'll get along somehow.

Pétain France can do without you. She has me! Pride is the most detestable of faults.

He goes. De Gaulle crosses to Yvonne as she enters.

De Gaulle He's a sad old man. Nothing and nobody can stop the Marshal on the road to senile ambition. Talk about *my* pride? Old age is a wreck.

Lights up as Pétain crosses to –

The cell.
  He sits on his bed.

Pétain (*to Pottevin*) That was the moment . . . the moment it all changed. When I made that crack about his daughter. I didn't mean any harm by it. It just came out. But there was no sense in apologising, it couldn't be unsaid . . . I can't tell you how much I regretted it.

De Gaulle (*to Yvonne*) I knew the Marshal wished he hadn't said that. (*Considers.*) But he did say it.

Blackout.

Act Two

Pétain's cell/the courtroom.
  Pétain, on his bed.

Pétain By 1936, National Socialism was in triumph in Berlin, Fascism reigned in Rome and Falangism was advancing on Madrid. I was in and out of the government. Monsieur Léon Blum became Prime Minister.

De Gaulle enters. Pétain stands. They are back in 1936.

Ah, de Gaulle. The Prime Minister has asked to see you.

De Gaulle Me? Why?

Pétain Can't imagine. Thought you might know.

De Gaulle Perhaps he wants to hear my views.

Pétain You're just a colonel.

De Gaulle Nevertheless . . .

Pétain Be careful, he's a lefty. He's against everything military. He leads the Popular Front, you know.

De Gaulle I know. And he seems to believe that the Maginot Line will protect us.

Pétain We've been through all that. For God's sake don't waste his time with that crap.

Léon Blum enters, on the other side of the stage. He is slim, dark-suited, a white handkerchief in his breast pocket. Sixty-four years old.
  De Gaulle enters. They sit in two elegant upright chairs.

Blum The King of the Belgians has today ended his alliance with France and Great Britain. A Nazi sympathiser.

De Gaulle I believe so.

Blum This puts us in great danger. The Maginot Line ends at the Belgian–German frontier.

De Gaulle My thoughts about this are well known.

Blum I'm interested to hear them again.

De Gaulle But for years, Prime Minister, you have opposed them.

Blum When one becomes head of the government one gets a different perspective. What would happen if Hitler marched on Vienna, Prague and Warsaw?

De Gaulle It's very simple. We shall either have a limited call-up or a full mobilisation. Then, peering out between our battlements and fortifications, we shall watch the enslavement of Europe.

Blum But . . . you wouldn't want us to send an expeditionary force to Austria, Bohemia or Poland?

De Gaulle No – to Germany itself. But we don't have that capability. All the aircraft and tanks we have under construction are for defence. We have no dive-bombers. The Germans have dive-bombers. They have read my books. They have mobile Panzer divisions. We don't. We need a mechanised army but it may be too late.

Blum Well, how the money is allocated is the affair of Monsieur Deladier and the War Department.

De Gaulle No doubt. But – (*Stands.*) Allow me to think, Prime Minister, that national defence is the government's responsibility.

He exits. Blum walks upstage to the witness stand.

In the cell –

Pétain (*to Pottevin*) People call me a Fascist now but the Socialists all spoke well of me at the time . . . Léon Blum called me 'the noblest of military leaders'. And he's a Jew, you know. Fortunately, he's giving evidence on Friday. He'll defend me.

Lights up. The courtroom.
Léon Blum is a changed man, now extremely weak and vulnerable. He stands up, not even leaning on his chair. A ceiling fan revolves. Payen stands listening.

Blum (*quietly*) In June 1940, after the invasion, the people were defeated and in despair. But they were told 'No, you are wrong. The Armistice which we are proposing, which dishonours you and delivers you into the enemy's hands, is not a shameful act, but a natural act which is in the interests of our country.' But the people didn't know the terms of the Armistice. And they believed what they were told because the man who told them was Marshal Pétain. He spoke in the name of his glorious past, in the name of the Army, in the name of honour. That is the heart of the matter. This was a vast, abominable breach of the nation's trust, and it deserves the name of treason.

Pétain, sitting on a chair, stares at Blum, shocked.

Payen But Monsieur Blum, were you not free with your praise of the Marshal on other occasions?

Blum I lived under the same illusions as the rest of France.

Pétain, weeping, stands up and turns to the audience.

Pétain Monsieur Blum was imprisoned and deported to Buchenwald. Then Dachau. I don't know how he got back. He seems to blame *me*. I'm a kind man, you know. Really I am. But those in command can never let kindness be mistaken for weakness. I wanted to kill those bastards like everyone else, but I had no *choice*. How do you think I felt about it? I felt angry! Fucking furious, that shit, that cunt de Gaulle taking all the credit, that's how I feel, I'm a soldier too, not a bloody saint! And he's no bloody saint either, all that crap about God's will, he's just too fucking ambitious and big for his boots, that's all, that's all there is to it. (*Fuming.*) I've never known an officer so detested. A contemptuous, patronising, intellectual snob, treating all who questioned his opinions as fools or idiots, always insisting that he was right. Like that argument about the Maginot Line . . . well, he *was* right about that, as it happens, as it turned out, but that's beside the point.

General Weygand approaches, leaning heavily on a stick. He stops, clicks his heels and bows to Pétain. Pétain returns his salute.

Payen (*or* **Clerk**) Would you like a chair?

Weygand No.

Payen (*or* **Clerk**) Please state your surname, first name, profession and residence.

Weygand Weygand, Maxime, General of the Army. Prison.

Payen General Weygand, how did you approach the choice between the Armistice and the surrender?

Weygand Surrender is shameful. Our Code of Military Justice lays down the death penalty for any leader who capitulates on the field of battle.

Payen But what did you imagine would be the effect of the Armistice?

Weygand I'm a soldier. Forgive me, imagination is not my strong point.

Payen Apparently not.

Weygand I prefer facts!

Payen Well, let me put it another way: wasn't the Armistice a capitulation?

Weygand (*rasping*) The Armistice was a heavy cross to bear, but it was also a weapon, the only weapon we had left. Would further resistance have been wiser? Maybe. But we were outnumbered. We were losing the battle of France. The war was already lost.

Lights snap: sidelight, across the front of the stage.
Sound: montage of loud noise. Air-raid sirens. Searchlights. Ack-ack guns. Maybe loud music with energy.

De Gaulle enters. He shouts across the stage above the commotion.

De Gaulle We must defend Paris! Street by street, if necessary.

Weygand (*having left the witness stand*) No. The government must stay in Paris and allow itself to be taken prisoner.

De Gaulle No. If you won't defend Paris we must leave – go to the empire. We have an army and navy there.

Weygand There is no choice. You must obey orders. I am in command.

De Gaulle Is that what you call it?

He exits as –

Lights snap back to courtroom and the sound effects fade.
Weygand is back in the courtroom. Silence.

Payen General Weygand, did you later receive a letter from General de Gaulle?

Weygand Colonel de Gaulle. Yes.

Payen What did it say?

Weygand The letter begged me to give the order to defend Paris.

Payen Did you?

Weygand It ended with these words: 'I send you my respects if the answer is yes.'

Payen chuckles.

Nobody writes to me like that.

Payen Did you consider arresting him for insubordination?

Weygand I had other things to do than bother about that great booby.

Lights cross-fade. A hotel dining room.
Sound: a cocktail piano tinkles. 'April in Paris' by Vernon Duke.
The dining room is huge, magnificent (if the budget allows) and virtually empty. Waiters wait, with little to do. Empty tables. Pétain is dining with Pierre Laval at a table set with silver on white linen. Laval is smoking.
De Gaulle enters, hesitates, then crosses to Pétain's table. Pétain looks up, surprised.

De Gaulle Excuse me, Marshal.

Pétain De Gaulle. What are you doing here?

De Gaulle May we have a private word?

Pétain You know Monsieur Laval, do you?

De Gaulle We have not met.

Pétain You have now. Colonel de Gaulle – Pierre Laval.

Laval How do you do.

De Gaulle (*ignores Laval*) A private word, sir.

Pétain nods, shrugs at Laval, rises and follows de Gaulle.

Sir – I beg you – the military establishment will never reform itself. General Weygand is a poor choice for Commander-in-Chief, he has never commanded troops in action.

Pétain He's an excellent staff officer.

De Gaulle But an Anglophobe. With political views on the extreme right.

Pétain A patriot, nonetheless.

De Gaulle Sir, do you not see? You are the only one who can avert the catastrophe of surrender.

Pétain You've changed your tune. Is this an apology?

De Gaulle No, sir. But France needs us both.

Pétain None of your superiors share that view.

De Gaulle Do you think I mind? I've always stood alone.

Pétain So have I.

De Gaulle (*carefully*) That's true. You have never lacked the courage to stand alone.

Pétain chews his lip, pulls his moustache. De Gaulle feels increasingly desperate.

If you don't make the right choice now, it's all over. I don't know how to say this, because it sounds so sentimental . . . but I admired and respected you like a father and I don't know what's gone wrong. Is it because of that book? Is that why we can't get together now? If only we hadn't had that pointless dispute . . .

Pétain makes no reply.

I blame myself for that. But you're growing older, sir. There's nothing wrong with that, but you must let go. I am the future, not you. Will you not trust me?

Pétain (*stiffly*) You're not speaking like a soldier.

De Gaulle stands to attention.

De Gaulle Marshal, I aspire to no greater honour than to serve you in this vital work . . . as soon as you decide to undertake it.

Pétain thinks hard, then comes to a decision.

Pétain No.

De Gaulle (*stricken*) No?

Pétain No. I'm not in command of the army. We must leave it to those who are. I cannot interfere. You must accept their authority.

De Gaulle So you'll do nothing?

Pétain On the contrary. I have been asked to form the next government.

De Gaulle's worst fears are realised.

De Gaulle But you won't, will you?

Pétain Why not?

De Gaulle What do you know about politics?

Pétain As much as you, I dare say.

De Gaulle Who will be in your government?

Pétain They will prepare a cabinet for me. Piétri. Marquet. And Pierre Laval wants the Ministry of the Interior.

De Gaulle Laval is a slug.

Pétain I know. It makes me shudder just to think of it. But someone has to take over this chaos and prevent anarchy. My country is calling me. It's my duty. Look, I have to go back, we're in the middle of the fish.

De Gaulle Your duty?

Pétain Look, let me give you my appreciation of the military situation. Boulogne has fallen to the Germans. One hundred and twenty thousand French troops were rescued at Dunkirk but their equipment is lost. Thirty thousand British troops are taken prisoner. The Germans are crossing the Somme. Soon they will cross the Seine and Marne. Mussolini will invade Southern France any day. True?

De Gaulle True.

Pétain So what are the military possibilities for continuing the war? Nil!

He tries to return to his table. De Gaulle, trying to control his emotions, stops him.

De Gaulle We have allies. In the eyes of the English, the Channel is still wide.

Pétain England won't fight now. They'll negotiate with the Reich within a week. Therefore the question is, how do we face defeat? I took victory upon myself, I will take defeat upon myself. I will deal with it.

De Gaulle But we have the empire. Syria. Lebanon. French West Africa. We could fly to Algeria. We could evacuate half a million men. We have some aircraft and some shipping there still.

Pétain I can't run away. What kind of military leadership do you call that, for God's sake!

De Gaulle I call it fighting on.

Pétain De Gaulle, when you are militarily defeated it is a false heroic to pretend you haven't been.

De Gaulle You won't fight on?

Pétain I will. But not your way. First I have to sign an armistice with Hitler.

De Gaulle That's not fighting on, that's surrender! Please, Marshal – old friend – please don't become Prime Minister. Don't accept responsibility for the defeat.

Pétain My strategy of defence must include surrender. Remember what I taught you? 'Defensive manoeuvres are not dishonourable.' 'Never launch an attack until the enemy is worn out.' Don't you see, that's my plan. I'm doing this for France.

De Gaulle For France you must not do this. You should stand up in your boots.

Pétain De Gaulle, face the facts. You're an idealist, I admire you for it, I always have. But I must avoid unnecessary bloodshed. I must keep France as France. Better that France retreats to Vichy than that it is completely occupied by the Bosches. I will do anything to see that no harm comes to Paris. That is why we have declared it an open city.

De Gaulle Londoners are willing to see London bombed.

Pétain Not Paris. No Frenchman is willing for that.

De Gaulle Please try to understand – that's not the choice! It's a choice between principle and compromise. If you compromise you will be a traitor. A collaborator.

Pétain Maybe. But if you leave, *you* will be a traitor. A deserter.

> *De Gaulle and Pétain stare at each other, their passionate lack of communication reducing them to a frustrated silence. Pétain issues a command.*

Pétain You are a soldier. I order you to stay. You must obey orders.

De Gaulle Great men disobey orders, when they are wrong.

He starts to walk away. Pétain shouts after him.

Pétain You're right. History will make one of us great. I know which.

De Gaulle turns.

De Gaulle History does not make great men. Great men make history.

Pétain (*simply*) I have made history. I saved France at Verdun, I saved France in the mutiny, and now I save France again. I am indispensable.

De Gaulle Graveyards are full of indispensable men.

Pétain I shall be strong, because I am right. And I shall do my duty to the end. I am not frightened to stand alone . . . but the people will stand with me, not you.

De Gaulle Remember this, Marshal: people get the history they deserve. Goodbye.

De Gaulle salutes. Pétain extends his hand for a handshake. De Gaulle looks at him for a moment, then exits.
For a moment Pétain is alone on the stage.

Sound: the Horst Wessel Song.
Tall red banners with swastikas fall from above.
Hitler (or a German General) enters.
If budget allows, German Soldiers ring the stage: live cast or actuality film projection.
Pétain turns, and offers to shake hands with the German, who responds with the Nazi salute. Pétain gives the French salute in return.
Photographers. Flashbulbs.

Pétain takes off his sword and hands it to the
German General as the music reaches a sombre climax.
Then it segues into the sound of kettle drums
beating the 'V for Victory' Morse code signal.

Lights up. A radio studio.
De Gaulle sits at the table in front of a BBC
microphone. The radio is on. Pétain's voice sounds
distant and crackly.

Pétain (*on radio*) It is with a heavy heart that I tell you
we must lay down our arms. I approached the enemy last
night . . .

De Gaulle switches it off. A BBC Stage Manager
hurries in.

Stage Manager Stand by in the studio, chaps. Thirty
seconds. General de Gaulle, speak when you see the red
light.

De Gaulle (*sitting*) *Comment?*

Stage Manager Er . . . (*In halting French.*) *Parlez quand*
vous voyez la lumière rouge. Stand by, five seconds.

The kettle drums stop beating.

Announcer This is London. The BBC calling France. This
is the six o'clock news on June 18th, 1940. In the studio
tonight is General de Gaulle, Under Secretary of National
Defence in the government of Premier Paul Reynaud.
Here now is General de Gaulle.

De Gaulle All you who listen to me in darkness . . . Has
the last word been spoken? . . . Must hope disappear?
Is the defeat final? No! Believe me, who speaks to you in
full knowledge of the facts and who says to you that
nothing is lost for France. Our immense forces have not
yet been put into play; we shall line up the necessary
number of airplanes and armoured vehicles; and the same
means that defeated us shall one day bring victory.

For France is not alone! She is not alone! She is not alone! She has a vast empire behind her. She can form a bloc with the British Empire which holds the sea and continues the struggle. She can, like England, use without limit the tremendous industry of the United States.

I, General de Gaulle, at present in London, call on all French officers and men who are now on British soil, or who might find themselves here, with or without arms, I call on all engineers and skilled workers from the armaments factories who are on British soil or might find themselves here, to get in touch with me. Whatever happens, the flame of French resistance must not be – and will not be – extinguished. Tomorrow I shall broadcast again from London.

> *If the budget allows: actuality film – the Champs Élysées. The Germans have entered Paris, marching past the Arc de Triomphe and down the Champs Élysées.*

> *Music: we hear the second movement of String Quartet opus 76 no. 3 by Josef Haydn. Melody: 'Deutschland über Alles'.*
> *In front of the screen – Pétain's cell.*

Pétain (*to Canon Pottevin*) On the 18th of June 1940 I was the most famous living Frenchman. I had my feet on the ground. De Gaulle had his head in the clouds. For de Gaulle, France was a dream. For me, it was the land, the trees, the soil. No, it was more than the land, it was the people. I loved the people. I'm a realist. The realist loves people for what they are. De Gaulle didn't give a fuck about the people. Never did. Still doesn't. How could I emigrate? How could *he*? I had to ask myself, am I doing the right thing? De Gaulle might run away but I, a true patriot, had no choice but to stay. How can you be a patriotic expatriate? How could that lunatic hope to

77

raise an army in England? I had to hold it all together till we could fight another day. So I signed the surrender. It was a lonely, bitter moment.

Pétain leaves his cell and meets a civilian. It is Pierre Laval. He is still smoking. Louche. Trilby.

Laval Hello again.

Pétain Who are you? I know your face, but . . .

Laval Laval. Pierre Laval, your cabinet colleague. Your friend. Didn't you know me?

Pétain (*irritably*) I knew, I knew! The old memory . . . Just a slip-up, you don't have to make a meal out of it. I shouldn't have signed it. I should have let those who lost the war surrender. I'm a hero, a symbol, the victor of Verdun.

Laval That's why it had to be you today. France called you.

Pétain It's funny, France only calls me when there's a disaster. It starts with flashbulbs firing at you. And ends up with machine guns doing it.

Laval No, no.

Pétain No, you'll see, they'll put all the blame on me.

Laval takes him aside.

Laval When I was authorised yesterday to ask you to serve as Prime Minister, you were granted extraordinary powers. May I congratulate you, sir?

Pétain Only as a martyr.

Laval On the contrary, you are now as big as Hitler, Stalin and Mussolini.

Pétain (*impressed with himself*) They're very big.

Laval In no time you'll be Head of State.

Pétain Head of State, eh? I've had a long wait, haven't I?

Laval A long wait.

Pétain At seventy-eight a Cabinet Minister, at eighty-two an Ambassador and now – at eighty four – Prime Minister. It's really quite an achievement, don't you think?

Laval I do. You should be very proud.

Pétain I am.

Laval One other thing. Something else for you to sign. Condemning de Gaulle to death.

He hands a paper and pen to Pétain, who hesitates.

I'm sorry.

Pétain signs.

Sound: Big Ben.
Free French HQ, Carlton Gardens, London.
De Gaulle sits at his desk, working. Every few seconds the doorbell rings. After three or four rings –

De Gaulle (*calling*) Yvonne!

Yvonne enters.

Who's ringing our doorbell all the time?

Yvonne People. They're bringing jewellery and donations of money for the Free French.

De Gaulle Ordinary people?

Yvonne Yes, we've had dozens of wedding rings sent to us by unknown widows. So that the gold might help us.

De Gaulle Widows. (*Blows his nose, wipes his eyes.*) These British. I admire and envy them almost as much as I resent them. It is a truly stirring sight to see each Englishman behave as though the salvation of his country depends on his own conduct. They are the people that I should have liked the French to be.

Captain de Courcel enters, his arm in a plaster cast.

De Courcel Sir. A letter from the French Embassy.

De Gaulle (*holding out his hand*) Quickly.

He takes it, and opens it hurriedly. Then he laughs.

Yvonne What's the joke, Charles?

De Gaulle No joke.

Yvonne Are they helping us at last?

De Gaulle This is a notification that I have been sentenced to death in my absence. By the Vichy Government.

He tears up the letter.

De Courcel We're all with you, sir.

De Gaulle Wonderful! Thank you, Captain de Courcel. Who am I going to fight with the help of a collection of one-armed cripples?

De Courcel looks at him for a moment, and then exits.

Yvonne Was that entirely necessary?

De Gaulle (*slightly ashamed*) No. I'm sorry. But . . . My God, I expected some result from my radio appeals. I expected to be joined by men of the Staff College, by officers, by Catholics. What have I got? Fishermen and Jews. Hoi poloi.

Yvonne Perhaps you won't despise them in future.

De Gaulle (*stung*) I don't despise them. I never despised them. It's just that those from whom I hoped the most have let me down.

Yvonne Not us.

De Gaulle No, my darling, not you! Well, what can you expect of a nation which elevates food, wine and fashion to the status of moral precepts? In last week's plebiscite nearly ninety per cent of the people approved of the Armistice. It's a democracy, he'll say. That's the trouble with democracy. I've never believed it a good idea to entrust the fate of a country to something that abolishes itself when that country is threatened.

Yvonne smiles mischievously.

Yvonne That sounds like something he'd say. We are supposed to be fighting for democracy. Aren't you being a little inconsistent?

De Gaulle It's all right to be inconsistent. I like trees, I also like woodcutters.

Yvonne Charles – how long can Britain hold out?

De Gaulle Long enough.

Yvonne Have you seen new intelligence?

De Gaulle (*tapping his temple*) Old intelligence. You just have to know history and the map of Europe. Ask Churchill. He's going to launch me like a new brand of soap. But he doesn't want France to play a real part in the war effort. The British are encouraging French soldiers to enlist in the British Army.

Yvonne I can understand their point of view.

De Gaulle (*appalled*) You can?

Yvonne Yes. You should try to.

De Gaulle Why should I change the habit of a lifetime?

Yvonne Charles, just be reasonable.

De Gaulle (*magnificently*) I am reasonable! It is unacceptable that France, alone among the great powers, should capitulate and opt out of the World War. It is a repugnant thought that a defeated France should be saved by foreign arms alone. It is not sufficient that some Frenchmen should fight on.

The Marseillaise, softly under dialogue.

Spotlights on de Gaulle at a platform with a microphone. His voice echoes.

Soldiers of the Free French Army: France must fight on! I am France, and I am fighting on. Since the war began, about one hundred thousand tons of French shipping have taken refuge in British ports – that means about ten thousand sailors. Several thousand soldiers wounded in Belgium are recovering in British hospitals. Most of you think only of returning home, the war ended. Those are Pétain's orders. But the war has not ended! The recruiting campaign is gathering momentum – we shall win!

Immediately a British Colonel replaces him at the microphone.
Music: changes from the Marseillaise to Elgar's 'Pomp and Circumstance March', No. 1 ('Land of Hope and Glory').

Colonel Gentlemen, welcome to the White City Stadium. A brief word from the British Government. We are only too delighted to place this splendid White City Stadium at the disposal of General de Gaulle. You have a free option to serve under his orders. But we must tell you, speaking man to man, that if you so decide you will be considered rebels by your own government. Whereas if you enlist in the British forces you will receive all the protection of His Majesty's Government while still being able to fight the common foe. You will wear British uniforms admittedly – but with an epaulette saying 'France'. I think that's pretty fair, don't you?

Lights cross-fade to –

De Gaulle (*to audience*) I liked Churchill to begin with. He was born for events on an enormous scale. He is a giant, a man of destiny, an indomitable warrior and, by the way, a literary genius. A man of my size.

Lights up. Ten Downing Street.
Three chairs. A side table, with a silver teapot, milk jug, sugar bowl, cups and saucers. De Courcel enters. De Gaulle looks at his watch.

But I was kept waiting for far too long at Downing Street.

De Courcel Is he keeping you waiting on purpose?

De Gaulle Of course.

De Courcel How do you know?

De Gaulle Because that's what I would do. He has a mastery of the terrible game in which we are engaged. He will try to throw dust in my eyes, talking about how we will work together for victory. But I'm not worried about victory. Led by such a fighter, Great Britain will not flinch.

He looks at his watch again, even more irritated.

De Courcel Do you suppose Mr Churchill can speak French better than he pretends?

De Gaulle I hope he can, because although I can speak English . . . I won't! It's a matter of honour. Roosevelt and Churchill are more dangerous enemies than Hitler – for unless France fights too, victory will leave the Anglo-Saxons dominant in post-war Europe, with France powerless and humiliated. (*He looks at his watch again.*) Clearly he thinks that I have come to Number Ten cap in hand. We'll see about that.

The door opens. Lord Halifax enters. His withered left hand is in a glove. Very formally dressed, black tailcoat.

Halifax Ah, *bonjour, mon géneral. Je suis Lord Halifax*, Foreign Secretary.

De Gaulle stands and shakes hands.

De Gaulle *Bonjour, milord.*

Halifax I'm afraid I have an apology to make. I'm afraid Mr Churchill cannot see you today.

De Gaulle Cannot? Or will not?

Halifax My dear chap, cannot, I assure you –

Halifax indicates a chair for de Gaulle to sit in. De Gaulle sits.

De Gaulle I hope that today we can finalise the terms of Great Britain's Accord with the Free French?

Halifax Great Britain's Accord with you, certainly.

De Gaulle No compromises are possible.

Halifax Has anyone offered you a cup of tea?

De Gaulle What would have happened to France if Joan of Arc, Danton or Clemenceau had been willing to compromise?

Halifax (*amused*) You compare yourself to them?

De Gaulle We shall get nowhere if I speak with false modesty.

Halifax Let's not bicker, we're friends. Tea?

De Gaulle A man may have friends, statesmen cannot.

Halifax Look at Mr Churchill. Milk in first? Look at the way he handles Roosevelt – he's patient, he's flexible . . . twists and turns . . .

De Gaulle He can. He sits on a solid state, an assembled nation, a united empire, large armies. I have no such resources, yet I, as you know – and don't deny it! – I am responsible for France. It is too heavy a burden. I am too poor to bow.

Halifax Be that as it may, you must understand that Mr Churchill cannot yet recognise you as France. All the world's powers recognise Pétain's government. Sugar?

De Gaulle makes a face. Halifax hands the cup of tea to de Gaulle.

Even the French Ambassador in London refuses to join you. He tells me that he cannot bring himself to join forces with a soldier who has broken his oath of allegiance and is proposing to lead an insurrection.

De Gaulle They will join me in the end. (*He stands.*) I have 'assumed' France. *La France, c'est moi.*

Halifax stands also.

Halifax No, sir! You force me to remind you that you are a virtually unknown colonel, a temporary brigadier-general who served for less than two weeks as Under-Secretary of War in the last days of a government that has now fallen.

De Gaulle And you force me, sir, to remind you that you were the architect of Mr Chamberlain's disastrous agreement with Herr Hitler at Munich, which sold the Czechs into slavery and which is why we are here today.

A tense moment, after which Halifax reverts to soft soap.

Halifax Be that as it may, we are prepared to recognise you as Chief of all the Free French, wherever they are, who rally to you for the defence of the Allied cause.

De Gaulle is not impressed.

De Gaulle What about those Frenchmen who don't rally to me?

Halifax Well, obviously you're not chief of those who enlist in the British Army, or who get jobs in British industry.

De Gaulle (*exploding*) This is intolerable! Everywhere I go to recruit French soldiers, your people arrive as soon as I leave and steal them back.

Halifax (*calmly*) They make a choice. It's for their own good. If they're in the British Army they receive the protection of His Majesty's Government.

De Gaulle If they enlist in the Free French they get my protection.

Halifax chuckles. De Gaulle is mystified. Halifax realises that de Gaulle was not making a joke.

Why are you laughing?

Halifax I'm so sorry, do forgive me.

Halifax takes a document out of his dispatch box.

I have here a letter of agreement from Mr Churchill. (*He reads.*) 'His Majesty's Government will assure the integral restoration of the independence and grandeur of France.'

De Gaulle Independence? Grandeur? Very nice words – but what about restoring French territory? And the French Empire.

Halifax Yes, Mr Churchill thought you might mention that. (*Takes another document out of dispatch box.*) So that there's no misunderstanding, here's another letter – top secret, not for any publication, is that clear?

A beat. Then de Gaulle nods. Halifax reads on:

'The phrase "integral restoration of the independence and grandeur of France" should not be considered to apply to the territorial boundaries of France.' But we shall, of course, do our best.

He hands the letter to de Gaulle, who moves away.

De Gaulle We have been fighting you for nine hundred years. Your triumphs have been our disasters. But there were no Englishmen on the Marne when victory was won last time, and yet again we have borne the German onslaught. You were not ready. You virtually disarmed in the thirties. You asked us to disarm. You took Hitler's word. You brought home in triumph a worthless piece of paper. Now Mr Churchill, a vigorous imperialist, has designs on our Empire. (*Reads the letter.*) Perfidious Albion. If there is one department I distrust more than the British Foreign Office it is the British Colonial Office.

Halifax I'm sorry you feel that way. Mr Churchill is doing all he can to help you. But he does want written confirmation of this understanding.

De Gaulle You may have it now. De Courcel, take down this letter please.

'Dear Mr Churchill, I acknowledge the receipt of your letters of August 7th, and I confirm that I have understood them. I take note of your interpretation of these letters. Charles de Gaulle.'

Halifax I'm afraid that won't be acceptable, Colonel de Gaulle.

De Gaulle General de Gaulle.

Halifax General . . . The Prime Minister wants confirmation of your agreement to these letters.

De Gaulle And I want him to guarantee that France's territorial boundaries will be restored.

Walks to the exit.

You can't push me around. Remind Mr Churchill that I have an Irish grandmother, good afternoon!

*De Gaulle exits with determination. De Courcel
hurries after him.*

Lights cross-fade to –

The Cabinet Room, Vichy.
    The French flag – and the Swastika, side by side.
    *Several Cabinet Ministers in civilian suits are sitting
around a long table. They include Laval, Pomaret, one
unnamed and non-speaking and General Weygand,
who is in uniform.*

Pétain Good morning, gentlemen.

All Good morning.

Pétain is handing out some typewritten sheets of paper.

Pétain First, here are some new laws for you to deal
with, Monsieur Pomaret. They were drafted last night by
my advisers. Sign them at the bottom and send them to
the *Gazette*. Next . . .

Pomaret (*interrupting*) Excuse me, Marshal. (*He stands.*)
I am the Minister of the Interior, not a staff officer. I have
never even heard of these new enactments, and the
Cabinet here has not debated them.

Pétain gives him a cold stare.

Pétain We are at war. That's enough. You only have to
obey. If I were told to wash the dishes, I would wash the
dishes. Sit in your place.

Pomaret sits, slowly.

Now then . . .

Weygand (*interrupting*) I must also make a protest,
Monsieur le President.

Pétain (*irritated*) Yes, General Weygand?

Weygand The government has been accepting breaches
by the Germans of the Armistice Agreement.

Laval (*to Weygand*) Don't forget we've been beaten.

Pétain Precisely, Monsieur Laval. Thank you.

Weygand But since I am referred to as our Minister of National Defence I had reason to believe that we were still resisting. (*He stands.*) Laval – you wallow in defeat like a dog rolling in shit.

Pétain Please! General Weygand. No unparliamentary language.

Pomaret stands.

Pomaret Excuse me, Mr President, but when were you ever in Parliament? And would you explain why we frequently learn of important decisions only by reading the newspapers?

Pétain I don't like long arguments. The Cabinet is not for debates. I have absolute powers. Everyone may speak on matters which concern his own department. Now can we get on?

There are sullen nods.

Next. We're changing our banner from 'Liberty, Equality, Fraternity'. It will now say 'Work, Family, Fatherland'. Is that right, Laval?

Laval nods.

Pomaret There is supposed to be a distinction between armistice and surrender.

Pétain has difficulty in keeping his temper.

Pétain (*picking up his papers*) The Cabinet meeting is concluded. You may go.

Pomaret and unnamed minister all exit. Laval and Weygand stay.

89

Weygand Marshal, de Gaulle is mobilising all the troops in the Empire. Chad, Cameroon, the French Congo and Gabon have rallied to him. Soon he'll have French Guinea and French Equatorial Africa.

Pétain Weygand, some instructions for you.

He hands Weygand a piece of paper.

Weygand Laval, did you write these?

Laval I drafted them. The Marshal approved them.

Pétain I did.

Weygand All political refugees to be handed back to the Germans?

Pétain makes no reply.

Sir, you are dishonouring our uniform.

Pétain Go to hell! Get out! Now!

Weygand exits.

Laval Marshal. I've decided to make a statement on the radio so that the Germans know my negotiations with them are real.

He hands Pétain a sheet of paper.

Pétain It says here: 'I believe in a German victory.' That's defeatist.

Laval A German victory is better than a communist victory. You want Stalin to occupy France?

Pétain Oh. I see . . . but don't say it like this.

Laval Very good. I'll rephrase.

Pétain And show me first.

Laval Of course I shall, Marshal.

Weygand re-enters with Pomaret.

Pomaret Marshal – a private word, please?

Pétain Pomaret, you can say anything you want in front of Laval.

Pomaret Sir, four thousand Jews have been driven back up into the Occupied Zone – seven thousand are in camps, waiting to be deported.

Pétain I know.

Pomaret Sir, I was at the indoor cycle track yesterday where the Jews are being held before they are put into cattle trucks and sent to the East. I don't think you can quite imagine it. The women and children, babies torn from their mothers' arms. Our police are helping with this disgrace.

Pétain suddenly weeps.

Pétain You're right. It is terrible. It is true that these Jews have not always had a good influence on the country, everyone knows that. But how can we ever redeem this? Never, never. And I cannot intervene without breaching the Armistice. I have no choice. But you cannot say I am anti-Semitic. I'm not discriminating against Jews. We are just as tough with the Gaullists and the Communists. Are there not tens of thousands of ordinary Frenchmen in prisons and camps for ideological offences?

Pomaret Yes.

Pétain See?

Pomaret is not quite sure how to reason with Pétain.

Pomaret (*gently*) Sir . . . You're an old man. Surely you don't want to present yourself to God with blood on your hands.

Pétain I don't think I believe in God.

Laval Anyway, blood dries quickly.

He exits, to –

The courtroom.
Laval is in the witness stand. Pétain is watching and listening.

Payen Monsieur Laval, you rejoined the government on the 22nd of April 1942. And exactly two months later you made a notorious remark.

Laval I decided to make a statement on the radio, so that the Germans would know I was sincere in negotiating with them. My statement was to include the phrase 'I believe in a German victory'.

Payen The Marshal asked you to leave out that phrase, am I right?

Laval Yes. I substituted 'I hope for'.

Payen (*repeats to courtroom*) 'I hope for a German victory.' *You* said that, not the Marshal.

Laval Yes, but the Marshal allowed that to stand. Quite rightly. Because the whole sentence was: 'I hope for a German victory, for without that victory the whole of Europe will fall under Communist control.'

Payen You may stand down.

Laval is led out.

If the Marshal is willing to answer, I should like to know how he reacted when . . .

Suddenly, Pétain stands. He is at attention. He speaks, and his voice quivers with anger:

Pétain I reacted very strongly when I heard that phrase in his speech. I hadn't understood. I thought the phrase had been struck out and I was shocked that it had been allowed to stand.

Judge But what did you do about it?

Pétain is silent. Then he crosses back to sit on his bed as lights cross-fade to –

A table and two chairs.
De Gaulle and Yvonne are having breakfast. Pétain sits on his bed, listening, watching.

Yvonne Are you satisfied with the way the trial's going?

De Gaulle Yes.

Yvonne Are you going there yourself?

De Gaulle That would be inappropriate. It could be seen as interference in the judicial process.

Yvonne (*surprised*) You mean, it's not a formality?

De Gaulle pours more coffee.

De Gaulle No.

Yvonne You have found impartial judges?

De Gaulle How can anyone be impartial about collaboration? We were the only occupied country in Europe whose government collaborated with the Nazis.

Yvonne I should have thought there might be judges who are impartial. The Marshal still has plenty of support, even now.

De Gaulle Yes. The people were forced to pick sides. That should never have happened.

Yvonne Some picked both sides.

De Gaulle Nearly everyone, as it happens. But now they all pretend they never supported Vichy – apparently everyone was in the Resistance after all, we just didn't know about them. Strange.

Yvonne And they all want revenge.

De Gaulle After a war, everybody wants revenge against somebody.

Yvonne (*contemplates him*) Do you?

De Gaulle As always, de Gaulle will do what's best for France.

Yvonne If Pétain's convicted, will you have him shot?

De Gaulle (*stands, then speaks*) God may be merciful but He and de Gaulle do not always have the same priorities.

He exits.

Sound: morbid drumbeats, like at the beginning of the play.

Clerk The accused will stand.

Pétain stands.

Judge Philippe Pétain, you have been found guilty of treason, and the sentence of this court is death.

Pétain does not move a muscle.

The judges have recommended a reprieve. This recommendation will be communicated to General de Gaulle. He will decide.

Pétain stands absolutely still. Then he salutes and returns to –

The cell.
  Sound effects: lightning and thunder outside. Torrential rain is now falling.
  Canon Pottevin is there. They are both sweating.

Pétain At last it's raining.

Pottevin So . . . now you know the verdict.

Pétain We all knew that verdict before it started. It was a show trial. That jury was chosen from my enemies, every one of them was a Communist or in the Resistance.

Pottevin The jury convicted you by only a one-vote majority.

Pétain It was a stacked deck, man! Judge Mongibeaux told everyone I was a traitor before the trial! Funny, he never told *me* that, not once during the entire four years he applied all the laws of Vichy. (*A beat.*) I can tell you, the liberation made me laugh.

 Pétain smiles bitterly.

Pottevin Laugh?

Pétain I was betrayed.

Pottevin (*astonished*) You were betrayed? By whom?

Pétain The people of France. Every day, every day of the war I went for a walk in the park in Vichy. Unguarded. Just a couple of police inspectors. Anyone could have shot me. The people love me, you see. And just before the liberation I went to Paris. Two hundred thousand people cheered me that day. They sang the Marseillaise. They shouted 'Vive Pétain'.

Pottevin I remember it. But it was the only way that Parisians could make a patriotic gesture against the Germans. You were a Marshal in uniform, a symbol of France's victory. It was not an act of collaboration, it was an act of resistance.

 Pétain laughs.

Pétain If that's what the people were doing, then everything I have done is also an act of resistance. You can't condemn me alone.

Pottevin You're right.

Pétain And we still don't know the real verdict. Whether or not de Gaulle's going to shoot me.

De Gaulle enters. They look at each other in silence. Pottevin leaves. Eventually de Gaulle speaks.

De Gaulle You know the judges have recommended a reprieve?

Pétain Yes? Will you accept it?

De Gaulle makes no reply.

Of course, you know that I should never have allowed you to be executed. That was just a trick, to make the Bosches think I was on their side.

De Gaulle I don't know that that's true.

Pétain Well, what's the difference now?

De Gaulle Stalin said to me: 'In the end only death wins.' But perhaps the important thing is that it doesn't win immediately. It's lack of religion that makes death too important. Death is only important because of what it makes us think of life.

Pétain Death's not important to me any more. If that's your decision I might even welcome it now.

De Gaulle I see you've been confessing to the Padre.

Pétain Not confessing. Seeking consolation. Why did you come?

De Gaulle Because I knew that . . . if I didn't, I'd never see you again.

Pétain Because I'm to be shot?

Again, de Gaulle does not reply. Eventually –

De Gaulle I am infinitely disappointed in you. And . . . sad.

Pétain So, at bottom, between you and me, was it all worthwhile?

De Gaulle Was what?

Pétain Ambition? Success? Power? Joy, even?

De Gaulle You might as well ask, of what use is life?

Pétain Yes.

De Gaulle Thirty years ago the High Command was right about you! Right for the wrong reasons. You *are* a defeatist. You have no hope. You never had.

Pétain I did. I won.

De Gaulle Not this time. And the end of hope is the beginning of death. Without God it's not possible for a reasonable man to have hope.

Pétain In that case, there can never be hope – because it's not possible for a reasonable man to believe in God.

De Gaulle I believe in God – and I have always been reasonable.

Pétain You never understood *my* hopes. You never understood my *sacrifice*. France turned to me on the most tragic day of her history. They begged me. I answered. I inherited a catastrophe. I wasn't responsible for it. What do you think it was like for me? I, the hero of the last war, had to sign on the dotted line. I am a martyr.

Holds up his hand to stop de Gaulle interrupting.

I gave away everything I believe in, to save France. I gave away my soul. I took the guilt upon myself.

De Gaulle You seem to see yourself as some sort of latter-day Christ. A remarkable claim for a man without faith.

Pétain I had faith in France.

De Gaulle Not in *my* France.

Pétain Your France, forgive my saying so, has always been a figment of your imagination.

De Gaulle That doesn't make it any less great. All my life I have cherished an ideal, a vision of France. I admit that it's inspired more by faith than by reason. I see France as a princess in a fairy tale, or the Madonna in a fresco. If France behaves badly, I feel that it is merely a ridiculous error, due to the mistakes of the people and not the character of the country. France is true to herself only when she stands in the front rank. She must hold herself erect. France is not France without grandeur. France is not France unless she is great.

Pétain Are you pleased with the crowds who cheer you now?

De Gaulle Of course not. They cheered you too.

Pétain Rightly. Paris is still standing.

They gaze at each other.

You've won everything. You've saved our people, our honour, our empire – this is your moment of triumph. Are you satisfied at last – here you are, recognised as the legitimate government?

De Gaulle Are you so very pleased when someone calls you by your own name?

Pétain But don't you realise? If I had not signed the Armistice, Paris would no longer be here for you to save? I saved France.

De Gaulle No, I did!

Pétain I kept hope alive.

De Gaulle No, I did that!

Pétain She is intact because of me.

De Gaulle No, because of me! You are merely the victim of worldly ambition. That's hardly what martyrs are!

Pétain And you don't care for worldly ambition, I suppose?

De Gaulle There is a place for it, I admit. Napoleon was ambitious. And you know something else? Your guilt doesn't make the French people innocent. I wish it did. Do you think the Fascists are not still here? As for the Communists, they were useful enough in the Resistance, but now they are trying to seize power, playing their dangerous party political games under Stalin's nose. He's in Berlin now – it's just an hour away.

    Stalemate. Pétain sits.

Pétain Did you want to put me on trial?

De Gaulle I had hoped to do it in your absence.

Pétain I'm not a coward! I made the Germans release me for this trial. The Swiss offered me asylum but I rejected it.

De Gaulle I know. That was courageous.

Pétain You're only in power now because *I put you there.* This is the letter I sent to Auphan.

    He takes a letter out of his pocket and reads it.

'From the Marshal of France, Head of State . . . I authorise Admiral Auphan to make contact on my behalf with General de Gaulle, in order to find a solution to the French political problem . . .'

De Gaulle You turned to me too late. The damage is done. You are a collaborator for ever. (*He crosses away, moved.*) How very distressing. May God rest your soul.

Pétain Are you carrying out a purge?

De Gaulle nods.

How many?

De Gaulle The courts have pronounced over two thousand death sentences. I think that except for about a hundred, they all deserve to die.

Pétain I see.

De Gaulle But I have reprieved thirteen hundred and three. And I have reprieved all the women who were condemned. Women should never be shot.

Pétain Members of my government?

De Gaulle Laval has been found guilty of high treason. He will be executed by firing squad. As will the worst of the others.

Pétain And what does France think about your purge?

De Gaulle (*sharply*) When I want to know what France thinks, I ask myself.

Pétain (*smiles*) You haven't changed, have you?

De Gaulle shrugs.

Have I?

De Gaulle stares at him.

De Gaulle Don't you know why I'm here? I'm here to try to understand – *how could you have done it?*

Pétain (*stands, angrily*) How could you? You spilt French blood. You turned it into a civil war. You made Frenchmen fight Frenchmen.

De Gaulle Civil war is no different to any other war. I had no choice. Good against bad.

Pétain Good against bad? Was it so simple?

De Gaulle makes no reply.

Have you never made a mistake?

De Gaulle Of course. A historic destiny is sure to involve many mistakes. But none so great as yours. You shook hands with Hitler.

Pétain (*passionately*) I attained power legally, with the overwhelming support of the French nation.

Sound: we hear the Marseillaise, distant.

De Gaulle No, sir. A nation is not the sum of its people. A nation is a myth. The existence of a nation is a matter of spiritual belief. And this belief unifies the people. Look at the Jews. A state is a fact – but a nation is just a notion. So when *you* say France, you mean all those people out there in berets, smelling of garlic. But when *I* say France I don't include those vulgar cowardly plebeians in the streets, I mean the Resistance, the best of France and the French from Charlemagne to Joan of Arc to Napoleon, commemorated and immortalised. What Britain means to Churchill. A nation must have pride! Many of today's French are a squalid interlude between the glorious dead and those yet unborn. If the people have no pride, there is no nation.

Pétain nods, and sits.

You had an obligation to tomorrow's people too. You were the trustee of a myth, not merely of what the people wanted. Anyone can give the people what they want. That is a contemptible ambition in itself. You should have aimed higher.

Pétain understands at last. He is weeping.

Pétain I see.

De Gaulle You just wanted to be President. Like all politicians, you posed as the servant in order to become the master. Look where your senile ambition has led.

Tragic music has returned.

Pétain Of course I wanted to be President. I don't deny that. Who doesn't? You do! But it wasn't just *folie de grandeur*. I am a patriot too. You were the sword but I was the shield. I love France. I also love you – my son.

De Gaulle I'm not your son.

Pétain You always were a son to me.

De Gaulle Perhaps. But I don't love you.

Pétain I don't believe that.

They are both profoundly moved. Suddenly they embrace, then they part. De Gaulle walks to the door.

De Gaulle I shall reprieve you, of course. However, I'm afraid that you will be exiled for the rest of your life. To the island of Yeu.

Pétain To die in Paris is the only joy I asked God to grant. (*Smiles wryly.*) That'll teach me. Well . . . it doesn't make much difference. (*Trying not to weep.*) Napoleon finished up in exile on an island, too.

De Gaulle You will not be remembered like him. Your name will be reviled.

Pétain Is that fair?

De Gaulle Yes. (*Unbearably moved.*) I'm sorry to say it is.

Pétain Will I be buried there?

De Gaulle I don't care where you're buried.

Pétain Where will you be buried?

De Gaulle I shall be buried with my daughter Anne . . . (*Wipes tears from his eyes.*) After a time we think of the death of those we love with a sweetness that cannot be explained. Perhaps it's because, now she's dead, she's like all the other children.

He turns to go.

Pétain De Gaulle . . . Goodbye.

De Gaulle My dear old friend, I had no choice in putting you on trial. I have no choice but to reprieve you. I can't sentence you to die.

Pétain No. You are sentencing me to live.

De Gaulle goes.
   Lights down on the cell. Lights up on –

A table and two chairs.
   De Gaulle and Yvonne are eating breakfast. Yvonne pours the coffee.

Yvonne You *saw* Pétain?

De Gaulle I did. There were some questions even I couldn't answer.

Yvonne Heavens!

De Gaulle It was terrible. 'Each man kills the thing he loves.' How true. How prophetic.

Yvonne But you didn't sentence him to death.

De Gaulle Not literally.

She understands.

Yvonne, I want you to pack. We're going to Colombey tomorrow.

Yvonne For the weekend?

De Gaulle For good. I have retired.

Yvonne Don't be silly, Charles, you've got a cabinet meeting tomorrow, it says so in the paper, look.

De Gaulle You mustn't believe everything you read in the papers.

He chuckles. Then he laughs. Yvonne stares at him.

Yvonne Charles . . . was that a joke?

De Gaulle (*still amused*) Yes. Wasn't it funny?

Yvonne (*with love*) In a way. But abdicating your responsibilities is nothing to joke about.

De Gaulle You sound like me. Yvonne, I chose my cabinet ministers fully aware of their stupidity. But they insist on voting against me. I hoped they'd be happy to do what they're told but they're so stupid that they don't know how stupid they are. They seem unable to grasp their triviality. I will not be manipulated by these political parties.

Yvonne In a democracy you always get party politics. It's in our constitution.

De Gaulle A constitution is like an envelope. What is inside it can be changed. Meanwhile, I shall abandon power immediately and they can fight it out. They are preventing de Gaulle from carrying out his mission.

Yvonne You mean you.

De Gaulle Of course.

Yvonne Have you any idea what it's like to eat breakfast every morning with a man who refers to himself in the third person?

De Gaulle Surely you know that when I say de Gaulle I mean 'de Gaulle'.

He indicates a mythical figure out there. She nods.

I will not allow them to discredit me. There will come a day when France once again needs a pure image, and I shall be ready. When I return one day I shall create a new constitution for me and for France.

Yvonne You can't create a constitution for you. You are not immortal.

De Gaulle That has yet to be proved. (*He chuckles.*) I saved France because I wouldn't compromise with the Fascists. They haven't gone. They'll be back. For now, I won't compromise with the Communists. That's not abdicating.

Yvonne Pétain has been sent to the Isle of Yeu – and you are going to Colombey. So you both finish up in exile?

De Gaulle The people no longer want either of us.

Yvonne It's so unlike you to give up.

De Gaulle I *never* give up. I'm doing what Pétain taught me. I cannot win at the moment – so I'm retreating until I can.

He leaves the table. Yvonne watches him for a moment.

Yvonne Charles, answer me truly – are you sorry the war is over?

He thinks for a moment.

De Gaulle War is horrible. But peace is exasperating. I feel bitter that the French people, who trusted Pétain, still won't trust me. And yet I won the war for them. I stood alone, you know.

Yvonne I know! I'm your wife!

De Gaulle France, ignominiously defeated in six weeks, is now one of the victors: there will be a French zone in Germany, we have one of only five permanent seats –

De Gaulle/Yvonne (*she knows*) – at the United Nations Security Council –

Yvonne I know!

De Gaulle – and with a veto! I did that.

He walks away.

Yvonne But the trouble is, you want gratitude.

He turns. Like a small boy, he is forced to admit the truth to her.

De Gaulle Yes. I do.

Yvonne You want to be king.

She has hit the nail on the head.

De Gaulle You think that's unreasonable?

Yvonne I think it's unrealistic. But that's why I love you.

De Gaulle Why?

Yvonne Because you're human. You're fallible.

He looks around cautiously, and then turns back to her.

De Gaulle Don't let it get around.

He chuckles, then kisses her and crosses away from her.

The stage clears. Nothing but trees. Greenery. Birdsong.
    We are back in –

The garden at Colombey.

De Gaulle (*to the audience*) I couldn't wait to get back to Colombey. From my study window I can look westwards for ten miles, and there is not one building in sight. The perfect view. Ten miles of France, and not one single Frenchman.

Pétain enters. He and de Gaulle stand side by side looking up at the chestnut trees.

Pétain (*to the audience*) Until the day I die, I'll always remember a conversation we had at Colombey, in his garden, years ago, when we still loved each other.

De Gaulle Chestnuts, eh? Beautiful.

They look at the trees. De Gaulle takes Pétain by the arm.

We're both rooted in France. Like them. Did I ever tell you the story of Bismarck and Moltke?

Pétain No.

De Gaulle 'After such happening,' Bismarck said, 'does anything remain that makes it worthwhile to have lived?' And Moltke said, 'Yes, Your Excellency.' He was eighty years old. 'To watch a tree grow tall.'

They look at each other with affection, then look back up at the trees.

Lights fade to blackout.

Afterwards

De Gaulle retired to Colombey to write his war memoirs, a classic of French Literature in three volumes. In May 1958, when France was threatened with civil war because of the insurrection in Algeria, de Gaulle returned to power.

He demanded, and was given, special powers. He resolved the war by negotiating independence for Algeria. He rewrote the constitution and created the Fifth Republic, in which the President was henceforth elected by direct vote with universal suffrage. He refused to support the US war in Vietnam, withdrew France from the NATO military alliance because he didn't want France to be dependent for its defence on other countries, especially Britain or America, and therefore insisted on a French independent nuclear weapon. He restored good relations with Germany and sought a détente with the Soviet Union, which could not be sustained after the USSR invaded Prague in 1968. He used the EEC to serve French interests, opposed a supra-national Europe and despised the European Commission.

In May 1968 there were mass demonstrations and student strikes, attributed to his autocratic style. In 1969, after thirteen years in power, he was defeated in a referendum in which he had proposed further government reforms and retired immediately to Colombey once more, to complete his war memoirs. He died before he could do so, in 1970.

The constitution he gave France survives today.

Churchill said of de Gaulle: 'A great man? Why, he's selfish, he's arrogant, he thinks he's the centre of the universe, he . . . You're right, he's a great man!'

The best part of Pétain's legacy was de Gaulle. The worst is Marine Le Pen.

Doubling

Parts may be doubled for a company of six actors

ACTOR 1
Pétain

ACTOR 2
De Gaulle

ACTOR 3
Photographer, Canon Pottevin, Corporal
(Operations Room), Deladier, Manservant,
German General, Hitler (if he appears), Waiter,
BBC Announcer, Pierre Laval, Lord Halifax

ACTOR 4
Clerk (first scene and verdict scene), General Joffre,
First POW Officer, General Hering, Léon Blum,
General Weygand, British Colonel, Photographer

ACTOR 5
Photographer, Guard (Pétain's cell), First Cadet,
General le Gallet, Second POW Officer, Payen,
Captain (in café), De Courcel, Pomaret

ACTRESS
Photographer, Second Cadet, Yvonne,
BBC Stage Manager, Cabinet Minister

JUDGE
voice-off (possibly recorded)